MY KEY WEST KITCHEN

MY KEY WEST KITCHEN
RECIPES AND STORIES

NORMAN VAN AKEN AND JUSTIN VAN AKEN

PHOTOGRAPHY BY PENNY DE LOS SANTOS

KYLE BOOKS

CONTENTS

Published in 2012 by Kyle Books
an imprint of Kyle Cathie Limited
www.kylebooks.com

Distributed by National Book Network
4501 Forbes Blvd., Suite 200
Lanham, MD 20706
Phone: (800) 462-6420
Fax: (301) 429-5746
custserv@nbnbooks.com

Text © 2012 by Norman Van Aken
Photographs © 2012 by Penny De Los Santos
Book design © 2012 by Kyle Books
Endpaper maps © 2012 by David Wright

Project editor Anja Schmidt
Designer Two Associates
Photographer Penny De Los Santos
Food styling Mariana Velasquez
Prop styling Sarah Cave
Copy editor Sarah Scheffel
Production by Gemma John and Nic Jones

Library of Congress Control No. 2012944605

ISBN 978-1-906868-75-8

Color reproduction by Alta Image
Printed and bound in China
by C & C Offset co., Ltd.

DEDICATIONS

NVA: For Janet and Mama, as
ever... and Lourdes now. How in
love we are with you, too!

For Charlie and Emeril, "The
Triangle" rides on. A "touch of
grey" but smile lines deeper.

For Justin, who drove this book
and its vision far more than I did.
(You did!) Love, Papa.

JVA: For my wife Lourdes
and our baby on the way; I
can scarcely imagine what's
in store, and I'm immensely
grateful for it already. And
for my folks—for teaching
me their craft and loving me
unconditionally and always.
May our efforts here show
our love of family, food, and
Island Time!

FOREWORD
BY CHARLIE TROTTER

I know a lot of chefs, from all around the world. Many are disciplined and even brilliant, but some, and this is rare, are original. Norman Van Aken falls into the latter category. Above all, it is originality that sets us apart.

Norman is a true gastronomic pioneer, even a culinary pilgrim. As a self-taught chef, he is equally (and deeply) steeped in both James Beard and the classic European traditions of gastronomy. He found his true culinary love, though, in "the cuisines of the sun," naming his brilliant first book, aptly, *Feast of Sunlight*.

Food products from South Florida, influences from Cuba, Central and South America and an innate sense of structure and taste in terms for devising his creations have informed Chef Van Aken's highly personal take on cuisine. Plus, he has the intellectual wherewithal to seamlessly weave seemingly disparate ideas into a highly coherent culinary philosophy that has literally resulted into Norman's "new world cuisine." I suppose it also doesn't hurt that he is one of the best-read chefs in America, and he applies that learning to his craft. It's not just cookbooks that he swallows, but classic literature, political essays and biographies. Indeed how many chefs are equally intimate with *The Alice B. Toklas Cookbook*, Nathan Myrhvold's *Modernist Cuisine,* James Joyce's *Ulysess*, and Henry Miller's *Tropic of Cancer*? Not a lot.

I think I speak from an interesting perspective. Norman gave me my start in the kitchen in 1982 in Lake Forest, Illinois, at Sinclair's Restaurant. His vitality and deep embrace of local and natural produce was quite eye opening. I then spent time with him in Jupiter, Florida, getting my first taste of the tantalizing treats of South Florida. Finally, and ultimately, I rejoined him at Louie's Backyard in Key West. His intellectual curiosity and drive to explore were more explosive there than ever. That influence is still with me today.

My Key West Kitchen is a remarkable book because it exudes the sensuality of the life and the flavors that Norman has discovered, embraced and refined for so many years. But here is where it gets even better: A young man, Justin Van Aken (no other identification is necessary), someone I even babysat as a lad, has partnered with his father to create this very special book. It's somewhat a father/son culinary love letter to Key West. Justin's passion for local, clean and pure product is most inspiring. He also possesses his father's keen and diverse interests, and has a strong but delicate approach to relationships with the pleasures of the table. Justin is a thinker and a doer in equal parts, innocent and focused at the same time. Enough, though, about the male Van Akens—I could, however, go on all day!

Most importantly there is the lovely Mrs. Janet Van Aken, who is the force behind the scene. In fact, she may be the best cook in the family! Her braised ribs, for example, should probably be served at the White House for the next State Dinner just to demonstrate true American culinary beauty. She nurtures, prods, recipe tests and does just about everything else to help keep those Van Aken boys in line. Had I met you first, Janet, who knows what I might have accomplished.

In the end, this magnificent work is so much more than a cookbook. It expresses the poetry, love and exuberance of all the things that make life worth living—family, community, the pleasures of friendship and of the table, and of reveling in the beauty of the diligence and passion that goes into achieving all of this.

I guess now I'm thinking about moving to Key West.

INTRODUCTION

The thing about Key West is that most of us knew that we were in love with the place. It wasn't just a place to live and work: It was our personal and collective Shangri-La.

Long before Jimmy Buffett wrote "Margaritaville" about Key West, we had already pledged allegiance to the magical little scrap of land at the end of the rainbow. We just felt lucky when we walked the old small streets and alleys, protected by some ancient maternal force. Something deep in our souls told us this was a place where we could find peace and quiet and a camaraderie of like-minded people. On top of that the city was stamped with a raffish charm, a *joie de vivre*.

You could remake yourself in Key West and no one minded as long as you helped keep the good times rolling. We lived day to day, but were intent to do it in quality drinking establishments and places to enjoy the crazy matrix of foods not eaten in most of America save, perhaps, New Orleans.

LAY OF THE LAND

When you come to Key West you soon learn that the island is divided into a few different kinds of geographical places. So often tourists only see Duval Street and that crazy, good-times action. We love Duval and kick off many nights doing what is affectionately known as "The Duval Crawl." In Chapter 1 you will be taken there.

But Key West is an island, and a residential one at that, and two other major *terroir* exist. The next area you will likely head to are places "On the Water." The sheer relaxation that exists when a human is well fed while staring out at the waters where the Gulf of Mexico meet the Atlantic Ocean is beyond mesmerizing. I spent four years at one of the most beautiful spots—Louie's Backyard. I learned some earlier lessons at a place I will always hold in my heart, too, The Pier House, where Justin learned to swim while I learned to sauté.

Then we have "In the [Neighbor]Hoods." These are the well-kept secrets that give Key West a charm that few find—but in Chapter 2, you will. Visit Johnson's Grocery in The Bahama Village to step back in time. Cross the street into Blue Heaven. Don't miss the Green Parrot; it's the most likely place you will find me and Justin chilling out.

My Key West Kitchen is, in part, the story of one chef's experience in Key West. It is also a snapshot in time—a time and place that was shared by a loose-knit assembly of artists, dreamers, travelers, workers, and the like—each of them true "Key West characters." These people came to Key West from faraway places—and many never left.

The collage of flavors from the American South, the Bahamas, Cuba and more are what I found when I arrived. In the ensuing 30 years I changed, I had a son, my son grew up.

In Chapter 4, "Around Town These Days," we will show you the Key West that inspires us still, and some of the great local spots we like to frequent.

RECIPE INDEX

SEAFOOD

Batter-Fried Shrimp Lou 2 27
Captain Tony's Sunday Fish Fry 32
Chez Nancy Lobster 44
Jerked Hogfish for "Big Bobby" 47
Shrimp Annatto with Cumin-Lime Butter
    and Smokey Tomatoes 53
Grilled Grouper with Mussel-Saffron Sauce 54
Crabmeat Enchilados 64
Whole Roasted Snapper with Anchovy
    Butter 78
Black Betty's Pan-Cooked Yellowtail 84
Catfish with Lemon BBQ Sauce 117
Mango BBQ'd Swordfish 118

SIDES

Cayo Hueso Cornbread 20
Tostones 67
Black Beans 163
Garlic Oil Roasted Potatoes 172
Janet's Fries 174
Yellow Rice 175
Cheesy Corn Grits 178
Blistered Corn 178

DESSERTS

Sunshine's Key Lime Pies 22
G.D.F. Cake 86
Caramel Flan con Coco 98
Honey Mango Ice Cream with Macadamia
    Nut Cookies 104
Georgia Peach & Pecan Crisp 144
Rhum Cake 146
Sour Cream-Vanilla Ice Cream 148
Justin's Best-Ever Peanut Butter
    Ice Cream 149

BREAKFAST & BRUNCH

Conch & Grits with Salsa Rosa 122
Tamale Scramble with Chorizo & Jack
    Cheese 131
Maduro Frittata with Queso Fresco 141
Soft-Shell Crab Pan Stew on Sausage-Stuffed
    French Toast 152
Golden Pancakes with Citrus Curd 154

BEVERAGES

Mamey Milkshake 16
Prep Room Mango Daiquiris 26
Café con Leche 38
"Woman Gone Crazy" Bloody Mary 39
Sunset Celebration 76
"90 Miles to Cuba" Rum Runner 77
A Cooler Full of Sangria 79

DUVAL AND DOWNTOWN CRAWLIN'

arrived in Key West for the first time in the Spring of 1971. The now-infamous Duval Street was nothing like it is now. You could roll a bowling ball down it in July and threaten almost no one. This was years before crowd-attracting events like Hemingway Days, the Bed Races, and the King Hell Daddy of them all, Fantasy Fest, had become traditions associated with the Last Island in America. Back then Key West was called Old Rock or The Rock, and the mixing of old Southern ways with Cuban and Bahamian cultures was established but in the most gentle ways.

In fact, Key West had always been an accepting place. When folks with peaceful preferences came to visit or stay, we were treated more often than not with friendly "good mornings." Although I eventually ran out of money and had to return to Illinois, the siren song of Key West beckoned me back with money I'd made in a diner up North in my pocket.

1973: THE MIDGET

In the Spring of 1973, I walked into a shack of a restaurant (even by Key West standards) and was handed a sea water–damp menu with items like turtle steak, jewfish chowder, fried bollos, tostones, guava milkshakes, and a meat dish, *ropa vieja*, that translated as "old clothes." Coffee was served in plastic thimble-sized cups and called *buches*. A mix of customers sat around the counter that morning: two rummied out shrimpers eating large steaks piled high with onions; a triple-tinted sun-glassed,

Bud Man gave me my first cooking job in Key West

stiletto thin, tense young Latin man eating nothing and watching the harbor; a "hippie-till-I-die" Janis Joplin–twin Earth Mama with a dozing baby; one rock-solid, leather and laced police sergeant finishing a Marlboro and a cortadito (Cuban espresso); a few dead to the world cats; a woman (?), bearing multiple tattoos and a shaved head; and a grand old Miss Havisham-type gal, replete with a conch pink–colored parasol who offered to read my palm. As fate would have it, I sat down next to a gentle goateed mountain that I came to know as "Bud Man." He offered me a job cooking ribs, Brunswick stew and chowder in an all-night, open-air barbecue joint about four blocks from the Gulf of Mexico, called The Midget.

Once I got started there, Bud Man introduced me to Bicycle Sammy, who had a voice raspier than Louis Armstrong's. Sammy was trim, almost muscular, despite his 70 years of age and he did not suffer fools gladly. Sammy had a bicycle that was his statement. The basket was large enough to hold a box of plantains or a case of shrimp. The horn was the size of a trumpet and could be heard from some distance. I worked the graveyard shift; Sammy's followed mine. Every morning he would arrive just as the sun was coming up, sound his horn, park his "steed" and, dressed in freshly bleached and starched chef whites, take over his kitchen. Sammy taught me how to say things like "Adam and Eve on a raft, float 'em!" for poached eggs on toast or "Shipwreck!" for scrambled eggs.

1977: 700 DUVAL

Janet and I were married in 1976, but to save up for a Key West honeymoon, we worked for a year at an Illinois country club before we could escape the grip of another endless northern winter. We still had old friends living in Key West, one of whom was a carpenter named Ricky Taylor. He'd been finishing the woodwork at a restaurant just across the street from where we crashed for those two glorious honeymoon weeks. Ricky walked into the Green Parrot Bar where we were steeling ourselves to face our impending return to our Illinois lives, lined up three shots with a Busch beer and said with his Alabama accent, "You want a job? Cuz if you do want a job, you ought to go talk to the guy I've been building this restaurant for. The chef he hired landed in the Key West jail last night and they found out he was wanted in Michigan on breaking and entering. That place is s'posed to open in less than a week and the owner is flipping. His name is Lou."

I walked Janet back to the house where we were staying and then headed over to the newly refurbished restaurant, which I called 700 Duval, after its street address (its actual name was the Lowell C). I found Lou, sitting on a barstool, sampling what clearly was not his first Planter's Punch out of a mason jar. I explained that I cooked. In less than twenty-four hours Janet was heading back to Illinois on a plane and I was heading to

BIRD'S-EYE VIEW OF KEY WEST, FLA.

Fort Myers with Lou to learn the recipes that he hoped would win the hearts of Key West.

We left Key West in Lou's big white whale of a Cadillac El Dorado on a beautiful morning. After completing the drive north out of the Keys, Lou turned west and headed across Alligator Alley in the early afternoon. Seminole Indians worked hand lines in the roadside ditches as if time had stood still. I stared into the waters and saw alligators pushing off the banks and marveled at the aquatic wonders of my new home state.

Tomasita Seafood, a typical family establishment in Key West

MAMEY MILKSHAKE

"Batido." *This pretty little word is well known all over Latin America and to many in South Florida as well. A sweet and frothy fruit milkshake, it's as varied as the currently available fruits in season. Guanabana, mamey, atemoya, coconut, cherimoya, banana, tamarind and many others—all contributing their gorgeous colors and enticing fragrances! Put the pulp of any tropical fruit or fruits in an electric blender with a little ice, a splash of milk and hit the blend button. Moments later, in a frosty glass, a delicious, healthy, delectable fruit smoothy is waiting for you. The buttermilk is my own addition. If you like the tangyness of sour cream ice cream or crème fraîche you will like this as well. If not, you can omit the buttermilk and go the standard batido route. It's all good.*

Serves 2 to 3, depending on your thirst

1 cup peeled, pitted and cubed fresh ripe mamey
1 cup milk
¼ cup buttermilk
¼ cup sugar or honey
1 dash pure vanilla extract (optional)
½ cup ice cubes

Combine all of the ingredients in a blender and blend until smooth. Serve immediately.

Ingredient Note: If you don't have access to fresh, ripe mameys, frozen mamey pulp can be found in many Latin American and Caribbean grocery stores. The flavor is nice though not as exquisite as the ripe, fresh fruit.

BICYCLE SAMMY'S RIB-MEAT CHILI

The Midget was known foremost for its barbecued ribs. One day Sammy got the idea to cut the meat off the ribs leftover from the night before and toss it in a pot of chili. Because most home cooks are not faced with loads of leftover rib ends, we've replaced them here with braised pork shoulder to make a chili that's just as flavorful but without the work of slow cooking on the grill and having to take the meat off the bones.

Serves 6 to 8

MARINADE
1½ tablespoons chile molido or chile powder
½ tablespoon cumin
Zest of 1 orange
Kosher salt and freshly ground black pepper

3 pounds pork shoulder, cut into 1-inch cubes
3 guajillo chiles, stemmed and seeded
12 ounces beer
½ cup pure olive oil or bacon fat
4 large cloves garlic, peeled and thinly sliced
2 jalapeño peppers, stemmed, seeded and minced
1 poblano chile, stemmed, seeded and minced
1 tablespoon chopped fresh oregano leaves
1 Spanish onion, diced (about 2 cups), plus more for garnish (optional)
One 15-ounce can tomato sauce
1 cup Java Gal's Lemon BBQ Sauce (page 167) or your favorite BBQ sauce
2 cups Black Beans (page 163), or other cooked beans you like (if not using our recipe, more stock may be needed)
Jack cheese, grated, for garnish (optional)

Preheat the oven to 350°F.

Mix all of the marinade ingredients together in a large bowl or zip-tight baggie. Add the pork and marinate for an hour.

Meanwhile, roast the guajillo chiles for 4 to 5 minutes, until they become fragrant. Pour the beer in a small pot and bring to a simmer.

Remove the chiles from the oven and place in a bowl. Add the beer and let the submerged chiles steep for 15 minutes to soften. Transfer to a blender, pulse until roughly pureed, and set aside.

Heat the oil in a large pot over medium-high heat. When hot, add the pork and cook until the meat is no longer pink in the middle. Add the garlic, jalapeño, poblano, oregano and onion and cook, stirring, until the onion is translucent, about 10 minutes.

Add the beer and guajillo mixture to the pork mixture and cook until the liquid is reduced by half.

Add the canned tomato sauce and lemon BBQ sauce. Reduce the heat and cook at a simmer until the meat is tender, about 2 hours.

Add the black beans and simmer for about 10 minutes.

Garnish the chili with chopped onion and/or as much grated cheese as desired. We often serve Cayo Hueso Cornbread (page 20) on the side.

Ingredient Note: Pronounced "gwah-hee-oh," this is a somewhat tough-skinned dried chile with a deep reddish flesh. It is obtained from drying a fresh mirasol chile. The heat is mild compared to many chiles with a tea-like flavor. Anchos are an acceptable substitute.

CAYO HUESO CORNBREAD

Like many things about our town, even the reasons for its appellation Cayo Hueso is clouded. The first part is easy: Cayo is Spanish for "key" or "island." But the hueso *part could have evolved from the word* oeste, *which means "west." (This makes sense since Key West is the most westerly island of the Florida Keys.) Or* hueso *could mean "bones," a reference to the final battle in the 18th century between warring Indian tribes who left skeletal remains on the beaches (these were quickly buried). The only thing buried in this dish is sweet corn and jalapeños, so rest easy!*

Serves 6 to 8

1 tablespoon unsalted butter, plus more for greasing
1 cup diced sweet onion
3 to 4 jalapeño peppers, stemmed, seeded and minced (about ½ cup)
2 cups all-purpose flour
2 cups yellow cornmeal
2 tablespoons baking powder
3 tablespoons sugar
2 teaspoons kosher salt
2 large eggs, well beaten
2 cups milk
½ cup vegetable shortening, melted
8 ounces grated pepper Jack or Cheddar cheese (about 2 cups)
1 cup Blistered Corn (page 178)

Melt the butter in a small sauté pan over medium heat. Add the onion and jalapeños and cook until the onion is just soft, about 3 minutes. Set aside.

Sift the flour, cornmeal, baking powder, sugar and salt into a large bowl.

In another bowl, beat the eggs, milk and shortening together. Add to the dry ingredients and stir just until the flour is moistened (the batter will be lumpy).

Stir in the cheese, blistered corn and onion-jalapeño mixture.

Grease a 9 x 13-inch baking pan with butter. Pour the batter into the prepared pan and bake for 25 minutes, or until a thin knife inserted in the center of the bread comes out clean. Let cool before serving.

> **Ingredient Note:** The secret to using chiles in cooking is to know each type well, handle it with care and apply its sting in concert with other flavors. Chiles are much hotter when they are fresh and take on entirely different characteristics when they are air-dried and/or dried by smoke. The majority of the heat in a chile is contained in the seeds and veins.

THE MIDGET'S BRUNSWICK STEW

One of the first meals I learned to cook at the Midget was its infamous Brunswick Stew. It is fairly well known that the original Brunswick Stew was made from squirrel meat. Lucky for you, I was all out of squirrels the day I made mine for this book, so I switched to chicken.

Serves 6 to 8

SPICE RUB
1 teaspoon black pepper, plus more for seasoning
1 teaspoon kosher salt, plus more for seasoning
½ teaspoon paprika
¼ teaspoon ground ginger
¼ teaspoon ground mace

8 bone-in chicken thighs, rinsed and patted dry
3 tablespoons unsalted butter
¼ cup pure olive oil
3 cloves garlic, thinly sliced
1 jalapeño (or other fresh chile), stemmed, seeded and minced
1 cup diced onions
1 red bell pepper, diced
1 cup diced inner stalks celery
½ bulb fennel, cleaned and diced (optional)
⅓ cup all-purpose flour
3 cups Chicken Stock (page 161), hot
2 cups tomatoes, peeled and chopped
2 tablespoons Pickapeppa sauce
2¼ cups cooked lima beans
2 cups Blistered Corn (page 178)

Preheat the oven to 350°F.

In a small bowl, mix the spices well. Season the chicken parts all over.

Heat the butter and oil in a large ovenproof pan over medium-high heat. Brown the chicken on all sides and transfer to a plate. Add the garlic and jalapeño to the pan and cook for 1 minute, stirring and scraping the bottom of the pan. Add the onions, bell pepper, celery and fennel, season with salt and pepper and continue cooking, stirring occasionally, until the vegetables are quite soft, about 10 minutes.

Whisk in the flour, stirring to coat the vegetables, and reduce the heat to medium. Slowly incorporate the hot chicken stock, stirring with a wooden spoon. Stir in the tomatoes and Pickapeppa sauce, return the chicken thighs to the pan and braise in the oven for about 50 minutes, or until the chicken is cooked through.

Stir in the lima beans and corn and place on the stovetop over medium heat until the stew is heated through.

SUNSHINE'S KEY LIME PIES

The first time I saw a key lime pie was a few days after I started at the Midget. It was about eight A.M. and I was having a cold beer, reading a newspaper, and getting ready to go home to bed. I noticed a young lady named Sunshine arriving through the doorless bar on her bicycle, wearing a cotton barely-there dress, a large hibiscus flower behind her left ear and bearing a tray containing two pale yellow pies. She explained that she only prepared two at a time or the taste would "get lost"; besides, she only had room for two pies in her bicycle basket. I drained the beer and saved my pie for later. (By the way, Sunshine went on to manage some business affairs for a guy named Jimmy Buffett, so she probably makes pies only for pleasure now.)

Yield: 2 pies (of course!)

CRUST
¾ cup sliced almonds, lightly pan-toasted
One 4.8-ounce package graham crackers,
crushed in the bag
½ cup sugar
1 teaspoon cinnamon
1 teaspoon nutmeg
⅔ cup unsalted butter, melted

Two 14-ounce cans sweetened condensed milk
One 12-ounce bottle key lime juice
10 extra-large egg yolks
(reserve the clean whites for the meringue)

SWISS MERINGUE
2 cups granulated sugar
1 cup egg whites
Pinch kosher salt

Place the almonds in a food processor and pulse a few times. Add the graham cracker crumbs, sugar, cinnamon and nutmeg. Pulse until well ground, but not quite dust. The mixture can be kept in the refrigerator for up to a week if not using right away.

Transfer the mixture to a large bowl and add the melted butter to combine. Divide evenly between 2 pie pans. Press the crust firmly onto the bottoms and up the sides of the pans, making a small rim. Bake the crusts until bubbling and turning from shiny to matte, 10 to 12 minutes. Cool in the pans on a wire rack.

Pour the condensed milk into a large bowl and stir in the key lime juice. In another large bowl, whisk the egg yolks until pale yellow Add the key lime mixture, stir well and pour into the pie crusts. Tap the pans on the countertop to remove any air bubbles and bake for about 15 minutes, rotating halfway through the baking time. Let the pies cool to room temperature, then wrap and refrigerate for up to 10 hours.

When you are ready to serve the pies, make the meringue. Set a pan of water large enough to fit the bowl of your mixer to a simmer. Add the sugar, egg whites and salt to the bowl and whisk gently by hand over the simmering water until the mixture is room temperature and you can't feel any sugar granules when you roll the mixture around in your fingertips. Transfer the bowl to its mixer and whip on high speed until the meringue turns bright white and holds medium peaks. Apply the finished meringue to the chilled pies. Torch at will.

Ingredient Note: The so-called key lime, a small, round fruit with a thin skin and a mottled yellow-green look, is, according to some, the "true" lime, Citrus aurantifolia. It is more tart than Citrus latifolia, the lime commonly found in the produce section of most grocery stores. Key limes are also known as Mexican, West Indian and Bartender limes. Key lime trees love the warmest weather and only grow down in the Keys in the United States. Trees were established as early as 1839. Gail Borden invented condensed milk in 1853 to give people in pioneer conditions safe milk that would keep longer than fresh whole milk. Some creative genius in the Keys combined sweetened condensed milk with key lime juice and eggs to make the first key lime pies. He (or she) would not be the last!

GREEN PARROT FRIED CHICKEN & WAFFLES

With my first paycheck from the Midget in my pocket, I sent for my girlfriend, Janet, who arrived a few days later on a Greyhound bus from Fort Lauderdale. With the remaining money, I found a place that would become a long-term part of my life, too: The Green Parrot Bar. The Parrot doesn't normally offer food (except the popcorn, which is free, like the live music), but every April, Green Parrot's "Head Spirit" John Vagnoni holds a party as part of The Conch Republic Independence Celebration Days. The G.P. team sets up chafing dishes on top of the board-covered pool tables and sells chicken & waffles. The monies collected go to The Bahama Village Music Program. The legendary jazz giant, some insist co-founder of Bebop, "Fats" Navarro was born in Bahama Village. He would have loved the Chicken & Waffles party. We all do. If you can't make it down, here's a recipe to import to your neck of the woods.

Serves 4 to 6

BUTTERMILK-HERB BRINE
1 cup low-fat buttermilk
1 tablespoon kosher salt
1½ tablespoons fresh lemon juice
1 tablespoon chopped fresh thyme
1 tablespoon chopped fresh oregano
1 tablespoon chopped fresh sage
1 tablespoon Dijon mustard
½ tablespoon freshly ground black pepper
1 rib celery, cut into large dice
1 clove garlic, roughly chopped

1 quality chicken (about 3½ pounds),
cut into 8 pieces
Canola or vegetable oil, for frying
Maple syrup, for drizzling

SEASONED FLOUR
3 cups all-purpose flour
1 tablespoon dry mustard powder
2 tablespoons kosher salt
1 tablespoon pimentón or sweet paprika
1 tablespoon roasted ground cumin
1 tablespoon freshly ground black pepper

CORNMEAL-RYE WAFFLES
2 cups cornmeal
¾ cup whole rye flour
2 tablespoons granulated sugar
2 tablespoons Belgian pearl sugar or more
granulated sugar
2 teaspoons baking powder
2 teaspoons kosher salt
1 teaspoon baking soda
3 cups low-fat buttermilk
2 large eggs
6 tablespoons unsalted butter, melted

Puree the brine ingredients in a blender. Place the chicken pieces in a resealable plastic bag and add the brine; refrigerate for at least 8 hours or overnight, stirring once or twice. Drain the chicken in a colander over the sink.

Mix the seasoned flour ingredients in a shallow bowl. Dredge the chicken pieces in the flour mixture, then transfer to a large wire rack to air-dry for 10 to 15 minutes. Dredge the chicken pieces a second time in the flour, shaking off any excess so it won't burn during frying.

Pour enough vegetable oil into a heavy frying pan to come a third of the way up the sides and heat over high heat until the oil reaches 350°F on a deep-frying thermometer. Starting with the dark meat, lay the pieces in the pan skin side down. After 2 to 3 minutes, add the white meat. (I like to keep the thighs in the middle of the pan where the heat is most direct since they take the most time to cook.) Continue cooking the chicken for about 10 minutes on each side or, more importantly, until an instant-read thermometer registers 165°F when the chicken is pierced at its thickest part. Transfer to a wire rack and keep warm by tenting with aluminum foil.

Make the waffles: Place the cornmeal, rye flour, sugars, baking powder, salt and baking soda in a large plastic container with a lid and shake well to combine. In a large bowl, whisk together the buttermilk, eggs, and butter, then whisk in the flour mixture. Let rest for 10 minutes. Make the waffles, according to your waffle maker's instructions.

Place a waffle on a plate, drizzle with maple syrup, add a piece of chicken, drizzle again and serve.

Cooking Notes: Since this is a brunch dish, we serve it with waffles and maple syrup, hence the salt level we call for is a notch higher. If you are preparing this fried chicken sans waffles, then you might want to back off on the salt a shake or two. The absence of sugary maple syrup is a game changer.

When cutting the whole chicken into pieces, I remove the backbone and wingtips and freeze them for stock making.

PREP ROOM MANGO DAIQUIRIS

Key West was a completely different world than Illinois, and finding cooks there was a completely different story, too. Then again, as chef of 700 Duval it was my first job where I was doing the hiring, so it was all new to me. Everyone I hired was older than me. One guy named Rick Lutz had been one of the original bartenders at the fabled Chart Room Bar at the Pier House Resort. When he applied, he told me he "had enough drunks whining about life's betrayals and decided to go 'behind the scenes' where the prep-kitchen work and rhythm were kind of close to making drinks." I wasn't going to argue—I was desperate for help. And it was hot and sticky in our breezeless prep room. One July afternoon, Rick rolled into the prep room with a leaking brown grocery bag, laden with burstingly ripe mangoes. He was whistling and clearly a little buzzed. He quickly and cheerfully set up a blender and his "bar," and in ten minutes had enough in the way of mango daiquiris to waste the entire staff.

Serves 2

2 ounces light rum
1 ounce Curaçao
½ cup finely chopped fresh mango
2 tablespoons fresh lime juice
1 tablespoon superfine sugar
2 cups ice

Combine all of the ingredients in a blender and blend well.

Pour into glasses of your choice. Serve with straws.

BATTER-FRIED SHRIMP LOU 2

When I became chef at 700 Duval, the owner, Lou instructed us to make a batter-fried shrimp using packaged Bisquick. After a few months, I refused to make it with that stuff. I had some "Mr. Natural" notion that there were unnecessary additives in that batter. I also wanted the dish to have some of the spice and flavors I was getting at a place run by some Thai folks down the block. Plus, the batter stuck to my hands as well—one night I lost my family ring in it and had to search the dumpster for it. In my anger, my frustrations became a symbol of the stupidity of this food. So I made up my own batter recipe. Lou soon found out about this transgression from one of the older cooks and he made a rare appearance in the incredibly hot kitchen to see if it was true. I admitted that I had altered one of "his" recipes and he canned me on the spot. I can't blame him; the dish was named Shrimp "Lou" after all!

Serves 4 as an appetizer

1 pound Key West pink shrimp (or the freshest shrimp you can find), peeled, deveined and patted dry
Canola oil, for frying

COCONUT MARINADE

1 tablespoon pure olive oil
2 shallots, thinly sliced
¼ cup red curry paste
1 cup fresh orange juice
One 15-ounce can unsweetened coconut milk
1 tablespoon fresh lime juice

TEMPURA BEER BATTER

3 egg yolks, stirred well
Scant 2 cups beer (or soda water, if you prefer)
2 cups all-purpose flour, sifted 3 times

Kosher salt
Lime slices for garnish

Make the marinade: Heat the oil in a medium saucepan over medium heat. Add the shallots and cook, stirring, until nicely colored. Stir in the curry paste and heat through. Add the orange juice and quickly reduce it a moment. Stir in the coconut milk and cook for about 5 minutes. Pour through a fine-mesh strainer into a medium bowl. You should have about 2 cups marinade. Let cool.

Using about ½ cup of the marinade per pound of shrimp, submerge the shrimp in the marinade for at least 1 hour. Reserve the remaining marinade to make the sauce.

Next, make the batter: Put the 3 egg yolks and beer in a bowl and beat until blended. Gently stir in the flour. (Do not over mix.) Keep the batter in the bowl over very icy water until ready to use.

Preheat a deep-fryer to about 360°F, or pour enough canola oil in a large pot to submerge the shrimp and heat until it reaches 360°F, as measured by a deep-frying thermometer.

With chopsticks, lift the marinated shrimp from the marinade, toss it in the batter to coat and gently drop into the hot oil. Cook until golden-brown, about 1 minute, then transfer to a baking sheet lined with paper towels. Season with salt.

To serve, cut each shrimp in half before placing into a serving bowl. Spoon some of the warmed reserved marinade over the shrimp or serve it on the side as a dipping sauce. Garnish with lime slices so guests can squeeze juice to taste.

Cooking Note: If you saved the shrimp shells, you can use them to intensify the marinade. Arrange the shells in a single layer on a baking sheet and roast them in a preheated 350°F oven for 5 minutes, then submerge them in the prepared marinade. Steep for 15 minutes, then strain off and discard the shells. Use the marinade as instructed in the recipe.

Ingredient Note: Four species of commercial-value shrimp are found in the Gulf of Mexico and South Atlantic waters. They are categorized by four major colors: brown, pink, white and royal red shrimp. The Key West variety are the pinks. These shrimp hide on the ocean floor during the daytime and come out to feed at night. The shrimping industry of Key West was still in full flower when we got to town; it only took a bucket of the steamed and chilled ones to make us fans. To my palate, their texture and sweetness are without rivals.

CONCH SALAD, MAN!

"Hey. Hey. I'm Frank, the Conch Salad Man. I'll sell you the world's best conch salad!" He was holding a huge white pickle bucket brimming with his conch salad. With no more explanation than that, he reached in and gave me a paper cup full. I tipped back a mixture of finely diced conch, tomatoes, red onions, Scotch bonnets, bell peppers, celery, citrus juices and herbs. The flavors of the sea were in there, too. Living in Key West was my culinary university; I never needed more formal training. The place was filled with honest, in-your-face flavors that came from the Cuban, Bahamian and African-American residents and wanderers who passed through. I didn't move to Key West to re-invent the cuisine—I came to find a home. In the process, I found a path to both. In this recipe, you will taste the foundation of each.

Serves 4 as an appetizer

1 pound cleaned fresh conch, diced
¼ cup fresh orange juice
2 tablespoons fresh lime juice
2 tablespoons fresh lemon juice
1 jalapeño pepper, stemmed, seeded and minced
2 tablespoons extra-virgin olive oil
1 tablespoon kosher salt
1 tablespoon chopped fresh cilantro leaves
½ European (hothouse) cucumber, peeled and minced
½ yellow bell pepper, minced
½ red bell pepper, minced
¼ red onion, minced
½ cup diced fresh tomato
¼ ripe Florida avocado, diced, or ½ ripe Haas avocado (optional)

Combine all of the ingredients except the tomato and avocado in a large bowl. Stir and refrigerate for at least 2 hours to allow the flavors to develop.

To serve, fold in the tomato and avocado. Transfer to 4 chilled glasses or serving bowls.

Ingredient Note: Those of us who have lived in South Florida for some time may remember when conch, freshly harvested from the sea, was readily available in grocery stores and fish markets. My first recollection of conch was watching young boys pulling them up onto the pier at Higgs Beach in Key West. A few weeks later, I learned to prepare a truly authentic Bahamian-style conch chowder using giant conch, or *Strombus gigas Linnaeus*, a mollusk that possesses a large "foot." They meander around on the ocean floor like aquatic peg-leg pirates, "jumping" and rotating to get food. The Bahamians taught us many ways to use this tasty creature and you can still sample fresh conch fritters, cracked conch, conch chowder and even conch carpaccio in Key West. If conch is unavailable, you may easily substitute shrimp in this salad recipe.

CARAMELIZED PLANTAIN SOUP
WITH SMOKED HAM & SOUR CREAM

The years rolled slowly by in the tropical heat of Key West. Janet and I loved the little town and we came to know the mix of cultures foremost through the food. We tasted a plantain soup at El Meson de Pepe (which used to be on Duval back then) and, afterward, plantains would never be far from my kitchen—they were the first exotic food I tried in Key West that just nailed me. What was truly remarkable was how they made all the other things on my plate so harmoniously delicious. At first I didn't understand how to handle plantains when I cooked them for us at home. I had no abuela coaxing me to "let them ripen, chico! Let them turn all black if you want them to taste the way you like them in the café." But you live and learn: I know now that the green ones are good for chips and tostones and the black, or maduros, *are good sweetly caramelized.*

Serves 4

¼ cup plus 1 tablespoon pure olive oil
2 tablespoons unsalted butter
2 very ripe plantains, skinned and sliced into
½-inch-thick pieces
Pinch each salt, sugar and cayenne pepper
½ teaspoon ground turmeric
2 leeks, cleaned and finely diced, white parts only
1 large carrot, trimmed, peeled and
finely diced
1 sweet onion, finely diced
3 cloves garlic, thinly sliced
1 Scotch bonnet chile, stemmed, seeded and minced
1 cup fresh orange juice
4 cups Chicken Stock (page 161)
2 cups heavy cream
Kosher salt and freshly ground black pepper

GARNISH
½ cup cooked ham, diced or shredded
½ cup sour cream

Add the oil and butter to a large saucepan and heat over medium-high. Add the plantains, season with the pinches of salt, sugar and cayenne, and cook, stirring occasionally, until the plantains have browned, about 10 minutes.

Stir in the turmeric, leeks, carrot, onion, garlic and chile pepper and cook until the vegetables are nicely caramelized, about 10 minutes.

Stir in the orange juice and cook for 2 minutes. Stir in the chicken stock and bring to a boil.

Reduce the heat to a high simmer and cook the soup for about 12 minutes or until the orange juice is reduced by half. Stir in the heavy cream, turn up the heat and reduce the soup for about 5 minutes, until it reaches a creamy consistency. Remove from the heat and, using a hand blender, puree the soup until smooth. I do not strain it but you may if you like. Season to taste. Keep warm.

Just before serving, stir the ham into the soup to warm it up. Ladle the soup into cups or bowls and dollop with sour cream.

CAPTAIN TONY'S SUNDAY FISH FRY

I received this note from Captain Tony's daughter, Little Toni: "We used to do a fish fry on the patio at Captain Tony's (Saloon) on Sundays—jewfish on Cuban bread! Had to do something with all that fish he caught! His favorite foods . . . hmmm. A piece of fresh fried fish with sliced tomato on the side. He really loved all kinds of good food, and of course, my mama's famous spaghetti and meatballs! XOX to you! Toni." Here's my take on their famous fish fry.

Serves 4

2 cups all-purpose flour
2 teaspoons baking powder
1 teaspoon kosher salt, plus more for seasoning
1 teaspoon black pepper, plus more for seasoning
2 large eggs, lightly beaten
2 cups beer
Vegetable oil, for deep frying
2 pounds fish, cut into 8 filets
Potato flour, for coating
2 tomatoes, cored and sliced medium thick
Cherry Pepper Marmalade (recipe below), as desired
1 lemon, cut into wedges
Tartar sauce (optional)

In a large bowl combine the flour, baking powder, salt and pepper. Whisk in the eggs and beer and set aside.

Fill your deep-fryer or a large pot with 3 inches of oil. Heat over medium-high heat until a deep-frying thermometer registers 350°F.

Scatter some potato flour in a shallow dish. Season the fish all over with salt and pepper then coat with the potato flour. Dip the fish into the flour, shaking any excess into the bowl.

Fry the fish in the hot oil in batches to avoid overcrowding until golden brown on both sides, about 8 minutes, depending on the thickness of the fish. Drain on paper towels.

Serve the fish piping hot with the sliced tomatoes, cherry marmalade, lemon wedges and tartar sauce, if desired, on the side.

> **Ingredient Notes:** Jewfish is now called "goliath grouper." But the odds of finding that fish in most of American markets is slim, so we use grouper most of the time. But fresh is the most important factor. If you can't find grouper, substitute snapper or dolphin. Potato flour is made from 100% ground dehydrated potato.

CHERRY MARMALADE . . . WITH A KICK

12 cherry peppers, stemmed
½ cup sugar
1 cup red wine vinegar

Pulse the peppers in a food processor until minced— you should yield 1 packed cup. Transfer to a heavy saucepan and stir in the sugar and vinegar. Reduce over medium heat until the liquid is all but gone, 20 to 30 minutes. Makes about ¾ cup.

DENNIS PHARAMACY NAVY BEAN SOUP

Reminiscent of the Illinois diner where I first met Janet was a little drugstore lunch counter called Dennis Pharmacy where they served good navy bean soup (the U.S. Navy kept Key West alive during the Depression), as well as a cheeseburger that got some notoriety over time. For my take on the soup, we prefer to buy a section of ham, bake it and use the trimmings along with the ham-hock bone to fortify the broth. Our kids need to know that meat comes from whole animals and each part of any creature we place a bull's-eye on should be used. It is a beautiful thing to slow-cook the navy beans and meat in a pot, watching how the slow dissolution of the formerly tough meat around those bones give way to an indolent perfection. Ever heard the phrase "The meat tastes sweeter close to the bone?" Now you can find out why.

Serves 4 to 6

NAVY BEAN SOUP

2 tablespoons pure olive oil
6 ounces smoked bacon, diced
1 Scotch bonnet chile (or other chile), stemmed, seeded and minced
3 cloves garlic, thinly sliced
1 onion, diced
3 stalks celery, diced
One 14.5-ounce can diced tomato
2 bay leaves, broken
1 cup white wine
14 ounces dried navy beans, rinsed and soaked
1 smoked ham hock
2 quarts Chicken Stock (page 161) or mix of chicken stock and water
Ham trimmings from a section of ham (optional)
Kosher salt and freshly ground black pepper

BAKED SQUASH

1 pound acorn squash, cut in half, seeds removed
2 tablespoons unsalted butter, melted
Extra-virgin olive oil
Kosher salt and freshly ground black pepper

Heat the oil in a large soup pot over medium heat, add the bacon and cook until just beginning to crisp. Stir in the chile pepper and garlic, turn up the heat to medium-high and add the onion and celery, stirring to coat with the olive oil. Caramelize the vegetables, stirring only occasionally, for about 10 minutes.

Add the tomato, bay leaves and white wine and cook until reduced by half, 4 to 5 minutes.

Add the beans, ham hock, chicken stock and ham trimmings, if using, and bring the pot to a simmer. Reduce the heat to medium-low and cook until the beans are tender, 1 to 1½ hours, skimming the impurities off the top as they arise.

In the meantime, preheat the oven to 350°F and make the squash. Score the flesh of the squash with a fork, drawing the fork back and forth over the flesh a few times. Brush 1 tablespoon butter on each squash half and season with salt and pepper. Place the squash cut side down in a roasting pan or heavy-bottomed skillet. Add a little water and bake for 30 to 40 minutes, until the squash is tender when poked with a knife. Leaving the oven on, remove the squash and let it cool completely before peeling off the skin and cutting the squash into bite-sized pieces. Arrange the squash in a single layer in an oven-proof nonstick pan, sprinkle with a little olive oil and more salt and pepper and heat in the oven until very warm, about 10 minutes.

Remove the ham hock from the soup and any larger pieces of ham, if using, and let cool. Carve off the good meaty parts, shred and return to the soup. If you have a good amount of bone and ham bits left over you can put it in another pot, top with cold water and simmer until it creates a flavorful broth. Use the broth to adjust the liquidity of the soup after you see how much liquid the beans soak up. A nice broth beats the bejesus out of water alone.

To serve, spoon the soup into warm bowls and add the warm squash.

Cooking Notes: If you chill the soup in the fridge and allow it to settle, you will probably notice that a fine layer of fat will form under the plastic wrap to greet you. You can skim it off if you prefer or leave it on and allow it to enrich the soup. Your call.

I love the smoky quality of the ham hock matched with the sweetness inherent in various squashes. (Try making this with kabocha squash sometime).

PLACES IN THE HOODS

The irresistible allure the Bahama Village section of Key West was a chance to learn what folks from another culture were cooking was made less daunting upon entering Johnson's Grocery at the corner of Petronia and Thomas Streets. My mother was born and raised in New York City and a fearless voyager her whole life; I'd like to think I inherited her sense of exploration. Time stretches a few generations back in Johnson's Grocery, a social gathering place. In fact, all of Bahama Village is almost an architectural museum, which has much greater visibility today due to the popularity of the Blue Heaven restaurant nearby.

Johnson's Grocery

Key West was the richest city per capita in the United States at the turn of the twentieth century but the poorest by the years of the Great Depression. Bahama Village was largely a black enclave and it was hit quite hard. The mostly small but wonderful homes stand just as they did in the early 1970s when I arrived in Key West, almost unchanged since the 1930s.

It has been said that "Key West is a quaint little drinking town with a fishing problem." Drink was never a problem at the Full Moon Saloon. We fell in love with the Full Moon Fish Sandwich that was invented there (and can now be found at Sloppy Joe's). If you didn't want to go home when the Moon closed, you could head over to the 21 Club in Bahama Village.

On mornings after nights like those, I woke and rode over on my Conch Cruiser (or bicycle) with bloodshot determination to a place I still love. It is called Five Brothers, at 930 Southard Street. Janet and I (and after 1980, Justin, too) must have lived in about 20 different houses over those years, most of which were near the Key West Graveyard, as it is the center and spiritual compass of Old Town, and Five Brothers is the nearby gathering spot.

1979 TO 1980: CHEZ NANCY

My time spent working at Chez Nancy was the first time I may have deserved the title Chef. I was reading like crazy; one of my bibles was the Time-Life series "The Good Cook" edited by Richard Olney. The Nancy of Chez Nancy bought me my first copy of *The Great Chefs of France* and it became the single most important book of that era for me.

I began to imbue the classic dishes of France with a tropical island identity—mostly because of the seasonal ingredients that were available in Key West. This way of cooking became a whole new vernacular in American cuisine, quite by accident.

I found another influential cookbook called *The Auberge of the Flowering Hearth* by Roy Andries de Groot that I found at Key West Island Books on Fleming Street. A small, inauspicious-looking book, it changed me and my thinking in fundamental ways. Mr. de Groot's work tells of the time he spent at a French inn in the town of St. Pierre-de-Chartreuse in Savoy. The inn was run by two women who created their menus completely from what the local area provided, from the aperitifs made with herbs growing on their grounds, to birds they shot and roasted on their spit, to perfect tarts made with the fruits harvested by their own hands. It was the single most perfect ideal of what I'd want my own restaurant to be.

1988: MIRA

But my vision of culinary glory culminated at the little jewel box of a restaurant my partner Proal Perry and I created within the beautiful Marquesa Hotel at the corners of Simonton and Fleming Streets in 1988. Proal thought of the name, MIRA, which means "look" in Spanish. We did more looking than asking to be looked at. Even so, the *New York Times* wrote about our food within the first month. And I finished my first cookbook in our office located in a former hair salon called the Beauty Box, a few blocks away. I also wrote a paper there called "Fusion" that I delivered as a speech, alongside Charlie Trotter and Emeril Lagasse in Santa Fe in 1988.

It was during the MIRA days that I got the message we were doing something different. Each morning I'd leave our home and go to La Farola grocery store near the graveyard. The old Cuban men still played dominoes in the back of the store where the cooking was done. I would get a large café con leche and Cuban toast, bike down to the Beauty Box and begin to craft my menu for the night, positioning a few cookbooks in one pile, my list of the foods we had on hand or that were coming in that day in another, and my "dream sheets," the partial names or ideas of dishes that entered my head as I went about my day, in a third pile. I wove together three or four first courses, three salads and six to seven main plates, trying to assign and divide the work out evenly among our small crew. Spanish Queso Soup with Spicy Sour Cream appeared with Hot Fried Rabbit Salad with Chipotle-Honey-Mustard Dressing, Torn Greens and Pickled Vidalia Onions; the Pan-Cooked Fillet of Key West Yellowtail with Citrus Butter was conjured in that office there and hasn't left a kitchen I've been in since; Grilled Gulf Swordfish with Creole Tomato Butter and Black Bean Salsa was another favorite.

I discovered another life-changing cookbook around then—*Culture and Cuisine* by the French writer Jean-François Revel—which it covered a vast sweep of culinary history extending from the 1300s to the modern day nouvelle cuisine movement. It inspired me to find out what I could about the roots of the simple joints in our town. I sat at the no-frills counters of most of these places and studied the menus, trying to discern how I might distill the honesty of home-style Conch cooking and fuse it with a chef-informed understanding of food.

CAFÉ CON LECHE

One would be hard-pressed to overstate the centrality of Cuban coffee in the day-to-day life of most Key Westers. There have to be about a hundred places to sit and sip the stuff. So, when in Cayo Hueso, do as the Conchs do, and start your morning with a sweet and milky café con leche. Or, if milk's not your thing, order a colada, a small cup (maybe six ounces or so) of rocket-fuel-strength brew that is so potent, it's often divvied up among eight to ten people. Serious stuff! For those of us that like a short, strong lift onto our feet after a rough night, the cortadito, at about four ounces or so, is a perfect compromise. It's the rocket fuel, cut with an equal proportion of steamed milk. The real trick to Cuban coffee is the cremita. It crowns a good café with a beautiful tan-colored foam similar to the crema on top of a freshly poured Italian epresso. To create this adornment, an impressive quantity of granulated sugar gets loaded into a small stainless-steel cup, filling it about halfway. In the Cuban cafés, it is brewed using a traditional espresso machine. At home, the coffee is brewed in a stovetop coffeepot called a cafetera. When you find a store carrying these coffeepots, they usually sell the little steel cups for the cremita as well. To make proper Cuban coffee, you will need both.

Makes 1 pitcher

Granulated sugar to taste
Finely ground darkly roasted coffee,
we like Café Pilon
Whole milk, hot or steamed

Place the sugar in a small pitcher. When the first drops of coffee appear out of the coffepot's spout, stir them into the sugar with a teaspoon, using just enough coffee to work the sugar into a paste and not a drop more. Return the coffeepot to the heat to finish brewing.

Meanwhile, work the sugar paste with the spoon until it becomes smooth and thick. You should hear a swooshing clackity-clack sound as the spoon whips the cremita into an emulsion of coffee oils and sugar. With practice, you will recognize good cremita technique by this sound.

Pour the rest of the brewed coffee into the sugar mixture and stir the bottom of the pitcher slowly until the cremita rises to the top.

If simply serving café Cubano, pour the sweetened coffee into small tazas, or espresso cups.

For cortadito, pour an equal portion of hot or steamed milk in with the coffee, see photo at right.

For café con leche, fill a small coffee cup with hot or steamed milk, then stain with the sweetened coffee to a pale tan.

For iced con leche, use cold milk and serve over ice with a straw.

> **Ingredient Note:** At some Cuban coffee stands, an old tradition of using evaporated milk still holds. This lends a silkier, creamier texture to the drink. Justin's wife likes to add a few grains of salt to the café con leche, a trick she learned from her Cuban grandmother.

"WOMAN GONE CRAZY" BLOODY MARY

For a few months in 1974, we lived on the second floor of a building that had been a bar for about a century. Known as the Red Doors for a long time, it had once been called "the Bucket of Blood," which points to a period of time when real pirates were part of Key West's scene. Caroline Street runs along one side of the building and Jimmy Buffett wrote a very fine tune about a "woman gone crazy" on said street. I was mostly crazed from low funds during that time period. We drank Busch beer and fished off the nearby docks with our hillbilly pal Butch to augment our meager dinners. Thank God Butch knew a lot more about fishing I did.

than

Serves 1

1½ ounces vodka
4 ounces tomato juice or 1 large
ripe tomato, blended
3 to 4 shakes Tabasco sauce
½ teaspoon Pickapeppa sauce
1 dash celery salt
¼ ounce fresh lemon juice
¼ teaspoon Sherry wine vinegar
Kosher salt and freshly ground black pepper
1 lemon wedge
1 celery stalk

Place a few ice cubes in a cocktail shaker. Add the vodka, tomato juice, Tabasco and pickapeppa sauces, celery salt, lemon juice, vinegar, a pinch of salt and a few grinds of pepper and shake well.

Strain into a pint glass filled halfway or more with ice cubes. Garnish with the lemon wedge and celery stalk.

Cooking Note: What will seem crazy about this recipe is the sherry wine vinegar. I ask you to make it for some friends—not telling them that detail—and see them react as mine did.

NASSAU "RUNDOWN" WITH SNAPPER & COCONUT

One of the most popular restaurants during the years I was coming up in Key West kitchens was called Las Palmas del Mundo on Southard Street. There was a tall breadfruit tree in the center of the outdoor patio dining area and the chef made a few Island-style dishes that take advantage of the generous tuber. A starchy, bland fruit the size of a football, breadfruit is not widely used in much of North America. Perhaps this recipe will change the tally by a few hundred or more. Though not needed to enjoy this dish it makes it all the more exotic . . . like so much in Key West does. "Rundown" is an island way of saying the sauce reduces or "runs down" the pot.

Serves 8

1 teaspoon ground allspice
1½ teaspoons curry powder
1 teaspoon crushed red pepper flakes
½ teaspoon kosher salt, plus more for seasoning
½ teaspoon freshly ground black pepper, plus more for seasoning
3 tablespoons fresh lime juice
2 pounds American red snapper (or other white fish), cut into 5-ounce fillets, skin on
Two 15-ounce cans unsweetened coconut milk
1 Idaho potato or ½ breadfruit, peeled and cubed
⅓ cup pure olive oil
1 Scotch bonnet chile, stemmed, seeded and minced
6 cloves garlic, minced
1 red bell pepper, sliced
1 yellow bell pepper, sliced
2 sweet onions, thinly sliced
1 cup white wine, such as Chardonnay
3 large ripe tomatoes, cored, peeled and roughly chopped

Cooking Note: The basic construct of this dish can be applied to a variety of ingredients—it usually includes fresh vegetables, some fish or chicken, and some starch brought together in a pot by sautéing the protein and vegetables with good curry powder, then deglazing, adding and reducing coconut milk-letting it "run down" the pot a while. Potatoes should be simmered in water until just done before adding to the pot. Bell peppers do best if sautéed first, then added at the end, just to heat them through.

In a small bowl, mix together the spices and the lime juice. Slash the snapper fillets crosswise through the skin and place them, skin side up, in a flat nonreactive dish and coat with the spiced lime juice. Let sit for 30 minutes or cover and refrigerate up to 2 hours.

Pour the coconut milk into a large heavy saucepan and cook over high heat for 10 minutes or until it is reduced to 1½ cups. Set aside.

Place the potato in a small pot, cover with cool water and salt to season. Simmer until just tender, about 15 to 25 minutes. Drain and spread out on paper towels to cool.

In a heavy-bottomed saucepan over medium-high heat, add enough olive oil to cover the bottom of the pan and sear the snapper, then transfer to a plate. Discard any oil from the pan and add enough new oil to coat the bottom of the pan. (You want to use the same pan to retain the flavors of the marinade.)

Add the chile pepper and garlic and cook for 1 minute, stirring. Add the bell peppers and onion, season with salt and pepper and stir and cook until the vegetables soften, about 5 minutes.

Reduce until the wine is almost evaporated, then add the tomatoes and stir. Taste and season with salt and pepper.

Cut fish fillets into bite-size pieces. Set aside.

Add the reduced coconut milk to the vegetables in the saucepan. Add the fish, cover and cook at a very low simmer for about 15 minutes, then add the cooked breadfruit or potatoes and simmer for 5 minutes more, or until the fish is cooked and tender and the stew has thickened and heated through.

Serve the stew over rice with lime wedges and Tabasco or another favorite Caribbean hot sauce on the side.

BAHAMA VILLAGE SOUSE

There are many definitions of the word "souse":

1. *to plunge (something, oneself, etc.) into water or other liquid*
2. *to drench or be drenched*
3. *(tr) to pour or dash (liquid) over (a person or thing)*
4. *(Cookery) to steep or cook (food) in a marinade*
5. *(tr; usually passive, slang) to make drunk*

. . . and many variations of the dish known as souse, as well. At it's most basic, souse is head cheese or brawn, a cold cut that originated in Europe, pickled in vinegar. In Key West I never had souse cold, but that is the way it often is served in Trinidad and many other places. When a fellow cook brought some souse into our kitchen in 1977 it was hot so that is how it is prepared in the following recipe.

Serves 8-12

PIG BONE BROTH
2 pigs feet, split
1 pound pig tails
1 smoked pork hock
2 onions, diced
2 serrano chiles, stemmed and minced
(seeds discarded, if desired)
2 tablespoons kosher salt
1 tablespoon freshly ground black pepper
2 bay leaves, broken
1 tablespoon pickling spice
1 cup distilled white vinegar
3 quarts cold water

TRIPE AND CHICKEN WINGS
1½ pounds honeycomb tripe, well rinsed
1 teaspoon kosher salt
½ tablespoon white vinegar
2 quarts Chicken Stock (page 161)
1 bay leaf, broken
2 serrano chiles, stemmed and diced, plus more for garnish
2 large tomatoes, peeled, seeded and chopped
1 small red or sweet onion, diced
2 stalks celery, diced
3 carrots, peeled and diced
5 cloves garlic, roughly chopped

First make the pig bone broth: Rinse the pigs feet and tails in several changes of water. Place with the remaining broth ingredients in a large pot and bring to a simmer. Cook over medium-low heat for at least 2 hours, until the pig meat is tender. Strain through a fine-mesh sieve, reserving about 2 quarts of the cooking liquid, and chill.

When cool enough to handle, shred the meat and set aside. (You might wonder about the fatty nature of the meat, but bear with me. Souse is a dish that unabashedly treasures the kind of fat that comes from the pig. Don't discard the beautiful flavors of the pig meat. There will not be much, but what will be there gives the finished soup what butter might to a more high-toned preparation.)

Cut the tripe into 1-inch squares, discarding any odd parts if necessary. Place in a pot with enough cold water to cover. Add the salt and the vinegar and bring to a boil, then drain and rinse the tripe well, throwing out the cooking water. Clean the pan and return the tripe to the pan with the chicken stock.

Add the bay leaf, 1 serrano chile, tomatoes, onion, celery, 1 carrot and garlic. Cook over a medium-high simmer, skimming as necessary, until just tender, about 2 hours. Remove from the heat and let cool.

In a large bowl, toss the chicken wings with the lime juice, salt and cayenne pepper; let marinate at room temperature for 1 hour.

Meanwhile, cook the potatoes in salted water until not quite cooked through, about 15 minutes. Drain and set aside. Heat the pig broth.

Heat the oil in a large flat-bottomed pot over medium heat. Remove the wings from the marinade and brown on all sides. Set aside.

1½ pounds of chicken wings, separated
3 tablespoons lime juice
1 teaspoon kosher salt
1 teaspoon cayenne pepper
4 to 6 Yukon gold potatoes, chopped
3 tablespoons pure olive oil
1 small red onion, diced, plus more for garnish
½ red bell pepper, diced
5 cups Pig Bone Broth
Kosher salt and black pepper
2 limes, cut into wedges, for garnish

Working in the same pot, add the serrano chile, red onion, bell pepper and 2 carrots; cook, stirring, until the onion has softened and begun to brown, about 10 minutes.

Return the chicken wings to the pot, add enough pig broth to cover, bring to a simmer, then reduce the heat to medium-low, cover, and continue simmering until the chicken is cooked through, about 20 minutes.

Add the reserved shredded pig meat, the cooked tripe mixture, the potatoes and warm through. Season with salt and pepper. Serve with the lime wedges and finely chopped onion and serrano chiles.

Ingredient Notes: If you have trouble locating pig feet and tails, ask your local butcher. Potato sizes vary; add only enough of the cooked potatoes as makes sense for your overall stock.

CHEZ NANCY LOBSTER

Grenobloise *(the French name for the classic preparation described below) is a sauce I learned from Danny McHugh, "The Irish Angel." How he learned it is unknown to me, but he often surprised me with his "chef's knowledge" despite never having been to cooking school. Danny gave me hope back in those early years of my cooking career. This grenobloise a great, versatile sauce for shellfish and breasts of chicken.*

Serves 2 as an entrée or 4 as an appetizer

Two 4-ounce spiny lobsters, cut in half lengthwise
Kosher salt and freshly ground black pepper
4 tablespoons Clarified Butter (page 180)
1 tablespoon unsalted butter
1 shallot, diced
1 bay leaf, broken
½ cup Chardonnay

GRENOBLOISE SAUCE
1 lemon, peeled
3 tablespoons unsalted butter
1 tablespoon small capers, drained and briefly rinsed
1 tablespoon coarsely chopped fresh flat-leaf parsley

1 cup small croutons

Preheat the oven to 350°F.

Season the lobster meat on both sides with salt and pepper. Set aside.

Heat a nonstick skillet large enough to hold the lobsters over medium heat. Add the clarified butter and lobsters and cook, turning the lobsters over a few times, for about 5 minutes, until they are nicely colored. Transfer to an ovenproof pan, meat side up.

Add the unsalted butter and shallot to the nonstick skillet and cook over medium-high heat until colored, about 2 minutes. Add the bay leaf and the wine and reduce until almost syrupy. Pour the butter sauce over the lobster tails and reserve the skillet.

Place the pan of lobsters in the oven and cook for 7 to 9 minutes, basting with the clarified butter once or twice to keep the lobsters moist.

Meanwhile, make the grenobloise sauce. Cut the white pith away from the lemon. Remove the segments by slicing between the membranes. Cut half of the segments into ½-inch pieces. (Reserve the other half lemon for another use.)

Add the butter to the reserved skillet and cook over medium heat, stirring, until it turns a deep brown and smells nutty, about 3 minutes. Remove from the heat and stir in the lemon pieces, capers and parsley; swirl the skillet to combine. Keep warm in a small bowl.

Remove the lobsters from the oven and transfer to warm plates. Spoon the grenobloise sauce over the cooked lobster halves. Scatter the croutons on top and serve.

BRAISED LAMB SHANKS WITH MUSTARD CRUST

"Braises are the philosophical cornerstone of French family cooking; they embody . . . or spark . . . something akin to an ancestral or racial memory of farmhouse kitchens, of rustic tables laid by mothers, grandmothers or old retainers."—Richard Olney, Simple French Food

After reading Mr. Olney's genius cookbook, I wanted to go more rustic than the rack of lamb I'd learned at the Port of Call. I would soon learn that Olney was a mentor to a woman who eventually became one of mine—Alice Waters. I was learning so much more about peasent cooking at that point like duck confit, pot au feu and pâté campagne. Buy the best bottle of Pinot Noir you can comfortably afford and enjoy it with this dish.

Serves 4

4 lamb shanks (about 4 pounds)
Kosher salt and freshly ground black pepper
¼ cup all-purpose flour
¼ cup pure olive oil, plus more as needed
1 cup coarsely chopped carrots
1 cup coarsely chopped celery
2 cups coarsely chopped onion
3 cloves garlic, sliced
1 bay leaf, broken
kosher salt and freshly ground black pepper
2 cups red wine
½ cup red wine vinegar
6 tablespoons tomato paste
1 quart Chicken Stock (page 161)
5 cups water

MUSTARD CRUST
2 tablespoons dijon mustard
Breadcrumbs, preferably panko

Preheat the oven to 300°F.

Season the lamb shanks with salt and pepper. Roll them in the flour, patting off any excess flour.

Heat a large skillet over medium-high heat. When hot, add the oil and sear the lamb shanks on all sides. Transfer the lamb to a roasting pan.

Add more oil to the skillet then quickly glaze the carrots, celery, onions, and garlic over medium heat to caramelize them. Add the bay leaf and season with salt and pepper.

Now add the wine, vinegar, tomato paste, stock and water to the lamb shanks in the roasting pan. Add the glazed vegetables and cover loosely with foil to allow some vapors to collect and braise in the oven for 2½ to 3 hours.

Remove the shanks from the roasting pan and place the pan on your stovetop over high heat to reduce the braising liquid by half. Pour the liquid through a fine-mesh strainer into a small pan and reduce over medium-high heat until the liquid lightly coats the back of a spoon, about 15 minutes.

Brush the mustard on the top of the shanks and sprinkle evenly with breadcrumbs. Broil until the breadcrumbs are just lightly toasted, 1 to 2 minutes..

To serve, place a shank on each plate and surround with the sauce.

JERKED HOGFISH FOR "BIG BOBBY"

Our fish in the MIRA kitchen came mostly from a guy named "Big Bobby" Elkins. He is still in Key West but doing real estate more often than free-diving with a spear to make his way. It takes some skill to spear a hogfish—while the body is large, the head is not and a fisherman does not want to put a hole in the body meat. After hours and hours of spearing hogfish, Big Bobby would deliver fish that still hadn't known a night in a cooler. I was working on various jerk recipes at the time, learning all I could about Caribbean cookery, and I liked to hand him a brown paper bag of his fish but "jerked" by me and my Sous Chef Susan Ferry back in those days.

Serves 4

JERK SEASONING
¼ cup allspice berries
One 1-inch cinnamon stick
1 teaspoon freshly grated nutmeg
4 Scotch bonnet chiles, stemmed, seeded and roughly chopped
½ medium red onion, diced
½ cup finely chopped scallions, white and green parts
3 cloves garlic, roughly chopped
3 tablespoons minced fresh ginger
1 tablespoon fresh thyme leaves
1 tablespoon sugar
1 tablespoon soy sauce
2 tablespoons Worcestershire
3 tablespoons fresh lime juice
¼ cup dark rum
Kosher salt and freshly ground black pepper

Four 6-ounce fillets hogfish
Extra-virgin olive oil
Good-quality salt like Maldon or sea salt
1 lemon, cut into wedges

First, make the jerk seasoning: Toast the allspice berries in a dry skillet until they are quite warm and fragrant. Transfer to an electric spice grinder with the cinnamon stick and grind. Transfer to a food processor with the rest of the jerk seasoning ingredients and blend until smooth.

Spoon ½ tablespoon of the jerk seasoning generously onto each of the fish fillets and marinate for up to 1 hour. Reserve any extra seasoning for another use.

Preheat the oven to 400°F.

Lightly oil a nonstick baking pan large enough to hold the fish in a single layer. Place the fillets in the pan and drizzle them lightly with more oil. Bake for 6 to 9 minutes, until the fish flakes easily.

Just prior to serving, season the cooked fillets with good-quality salt and add a squeeze of fresh lemon juice.

Ingredient Note: Hogfish is prized for its sweet delicate meat. It is found in abundance throughout the Keys as well as Bermuda and much of the Caribbean. Often labeled a "snapper," it is actually in the "wrasse" family.

TOURNEDOS, FOR A MOTHER

I was serving this dish at Chez Nancy when Janet was becoming closer to motherhood by the day. Tournedos, a term that usually refers to a pair of small center cut portions of filet mignon, are often linked to the inclusion of foie gras. We couldn't get foie gras except the canned stuff back then in America, much less Key West. And I was not about to introduce canned meats no matter how "gourmet" to the intended benefactor of this late-night feast after the heroic energies she had expended in child birth. So I took a page from the French in another fashion and cracked quail eggs, cooked them sunny side up and served them on the beef. Croque Madame is a rightful inspiration.

Serves 2

Two 5-ounce center-cut filet mignons
Kosher salt and freshly ground black pepper
1 tablespoon extra-virgin olive oil or
3 tablespoons Clarified Butter (page 180)
2 slices white bread (or crustless baguette),
cut into rounds
1 tablespoon canola oil, plus more for frying eggs
2 tablespoons plus 1 teaspoon unsalted butter
½ cup cleaned and sliced wild mushrooms, or
the best you can find
2 tablespoons Madeira wine
1 teaspoon sherry wine vinegar
1 cup Beef Stock (page 160), reduced by half
2 fresh quail eggs, or hen's eggs

Season the filet mignons with salt and pepper and set aside.

In a medium skillet over medium heat, heat the olive oil or clarified butter. Toast the slices of bread on each side. Transfer to a plate and set aside.

Using the same pan, turn up the heat to medium-high and add the canola oil. Sear the beef on both sides. Decrease the heat to medium, add 1 tablespoon butter and cook the beef, basting it a few times with the fat. Cook for about 3 minutes on the first side and 2 minutes on the second side, or until medium-rare. Remove to a plate and keep warm under tented foil.

Using the same pan, pour out the fat and add 2 tablespoons butter. When it's melted, add the mushrooms, season lightly with salt and pepper and cook over medium-high heat, stirring, until syrupy. Add the Madeira and sherry vinegar and reduce for 2 to 3 minutes, then add the beef stock. Turn up the heat and when the sauce is reduced enough to coat the back of a spoon, stir in the last teaspoon of butter. Turn off the heat.

Heat a small nonstick pan over medium-high heat. Add just enough canola oil to coat the bottom of the pan and fry the eggs sunny side up. Season with salt and pepper.

Place the toasts in the center of two warm plates. Top with the beef. Pour the sauce over the beef. Carefully place a fried egg on top of each piece of beef and serve immediately.

Cooking Note: Once you make this dish, you will find that adding other elements to the reduction sauce (a teaspoon of dijon mustard, for instance) can become portals to many exciting flavor combinations. Keep experimenting. It is how we grow in the kitchen.

SPANISH STEAK TARTARE MONTADITO SALAD

This dish was on the MIRA menu when we launched a prix fixe menu called "In Love with Spanish Flavors." That was back in 1988 . . . and the menu still holds up today.

Serves 4

TARTARE
½ pound completely trimmed filet mignon, finely chopped
2 egg yolks, stirred
½ tablespoon freshly ground black pepper
2 tablespoons finely diced red onion
2 tablespoon chopped fresh tarragon or Italian parsley leaves
3 anchovy fillets, rinsed well, patted dry and minced
1 tablespoon minced tiny capers, drained and well rinsed

SALSA
1 clove garlic, minced
½ cup diced red onion
1 teaspoon Tabasco sauce
1 ripe heirloom tomato, peeled, seeded and diced
2 tablespoons Sherry wine vinegar
6 tablespoons extra-virgin olive oil
Kosher salt and freshly ground black pepper

MANCHEGO VINAIGRETTE
1 to 2 cloves garlic, minced
¼ cup finely grated Manchego cheese
Kosher salt and freshly ground black pepper
2 tablespoons fresh lemon juice
½ cup extra-virgin olive oil

8 slices baguette, ciabatta or peasant loaf slices
Pure olive oil for toasting
2 small handfuls arugula leaves and/or mesclun (50/50 mix if using both)
1 radish, thinly sliced
1 small red onion, thinly sliced
Maldon salt or sea salt

In a large bowl, combine the meat with the remaining tartare ingredients and stir well. In a medium bowl, combine all of the salsa ingredients and season with salt and pepper.

Make the vinaigrette: Place the Manchego and garlic in a medium bowl and mash with the back of a fork to integrate the garlic. Add a pinch of salt and pepper and mash once more. Add the lemon juice, then the oil and whisk to incorporate. Taste to adjust the seasoning.

Brush both sides of the bread with olive oil and toast in a pan over medium-high heat. Transfer to paper towels to soak up excess oil.

Place equal amounts of steak tartare on 4 pieces of toast and a spoonful of salsa on the other 4 pieces of toast. Place the salsa-topped toast in the center of each plate and top squarely with the tartare-topped toast. Mound the arugula, radish and red onion slices around each portion, pour over some vinaigrette, sprinkle with Maldon salt and serve.

Wednesday, October 13, 1988
*****
Grilled Marinated Key West Shrimp with Chorizo Sausage and Tomato Chutney 8.50

A Mélange of Shiitakes and Golden Chanterelles on Wild Mushroom Toasts with a Vintage Port Infused Cream 10.00

Duck "Ham" with Chervil Pasta, Asparagus Spears and Cracked Black Pepper Brie Cream 8.00
*****
A Mesclun of Lettuces with Roasted Shallots, Diced Mango and Cabecou "Tartines" 7.00

Composed Artichoke à la Russe: Beet Vinaigrette, Sour Cream and Black Caviar 10.00

Pork Taquito Salad with Greens and Guacamole 8.50
*****
Grilled Yellowfin Tuna with Black Olive Purée and Beaujolais Caramelized Red Onions 24.00

Roast Rack of Lamb with Madeira, a Brunoise of Root Vegetables and Tiny Parsnip Pancakes 27.00

Ménage à Trois: Grilled Salmon, Tea and Lemon 24.00

Red Meat with Wine: Seared Rare Filet of Beef with Quail and Foie Gras Ravioli 26.00

"Fish House Fricassée", Lobster, Shrimp, Scallops and Clams Stewed with Vegetables and White Wine 25.00

Chili Spiked Veal Adobo with Pickled Corn Relish, Bean Dip, Tortillas and a Spanish Sherry Wine Vinegar Reduction 25.00
*****
Wines by the Glass

Early Harvest Gewurztraminer, Clos Du Bois, 86 5.00

Chardonnay, Neyers, 85 7.75

Beaujolais Villages, L. Jadot, 87 5.00

SHRIMP ANNATTO
WITH CUMIN-LIME BUTTER & SMOKEY TOMATOES

I was cooking at MIRA (now Café Marquesa) when I first made this recipe. The colors of this dish are as vibrant as the flavors, and one of which is the Annatto Oil you use here (and in many other places just as soon as you see how easy it is). It is a fraction of the price of saffron, too, by the way. I'm not saying it tastes the same but it is as pretty as the costly stigma of a crocus, or maybe better—as pretty as the colors you'll find in a Key West sunset.

Serves 4

ANNATTO OIL
1 teaspoon annatto seeds
½ cup pure olive oil

CUMIN-LIME BUTTER
½ cup fresh orange juice
¼ cup fresh lime juice
1 teaspoon toasted and ground cumin seeds
1 shallot, sliced
4 black peppercorns, bruised
1 bay leaf, broken
¼ cup heavy cream
5½ tablespoons unsalted butter, cut into small pieces, cold
Kosher salt and freshly ground pepper

SHRIMP
2 tablespoons Annatto Oil (above)
2 tablespoons unsalted butter
1 shallot, thinly sliced
½ to 1 serrano chile, stemmed, seeded and minced
1 clove garlic, thinly sliced
24 shrimp (about 1½ pounds), peeled and deveined
¾ cup fresh orange juice
1½ cups Smokey Oven-Roasted Tomatoes (page 181)

First, make the annatto oil: Place the annatto seeds in a clean dry saucepan and toast over medium-high heat until the seeds are quite warm. Add the olive oil, and when it starts to simmer, remove the pan from the heat and let the oil cool. Pour through a fine-mesh sieve and set the oil aside until needed. It can also be made a week in advance and stored in an airtight container in a cool, dry place.

Next, in a heavy-bottomed nonreactive saucepan, make the cumin-lime butter. Combine the orange juice, lime juice, cumin seeds, shallot, peppercorns and bay leaf and reduce over medium-high heat until the mixture becomes light and syrupy, 8 to 10 minutes. Stir in the cream and bring to a boil, letting it reduce just a bit. Whisk in the butter and season with salt and pepper. Strain through a fine-mesh sieve and keep warm until needed.

Heat a large nonstick pan over medium-high heat. Add the annatto oil and butter and swirl. Stir in the shallot, serrano chile and garlic. Reduce the heat to medium and cook until the shallots are softened and lightly golden. Add the shrimp and stir, season with salt and pepper, and cook, turning from time to time to cook evenly. When the shrimp are cooked through, add the orange juice.

Using tongs, transfer the shrimp one by one to a large bowl and keep warm. Reduce the juice to a syrupy consistency. Pour the reduced liquid through a fine strainer and drizzle it over the finished plate when ready to serve.

Dice the smokey tomatoes and place them on a platter in a 350°F oven to warm them up. Spoon the warm cumin-lime butter onto 4 warm plates. Distribute the shrimp on top of that and drizzle the warm annatto oil on top of the shrimp for added flavor. Scatter the smoked tomatoes around the shrimp and serve immediately.

GRILLED GROUPER
WITH MUSSEL-SAFFRON SAUCE

James Beard's cookbooks were growing in number each year during my time cooking at MIRA. In one of them, he introduced me to the basic idea of this sauce via a soup he helped make famous called Billi Bi, a mussels-based soup in which he used mussels, orange juice and cream. I just have loved it for eons so I decided to try to make a billi bi using coconut milk and cream. I have read many different accounts on how the soup got its name, but like many food stories there are believers and non—I am naming this after its central ingredients to avoid fistfights or rapidly typed emails.

Serves 6

MUSSEL-SAFFRON SAUCE
¼ cup pure olive oil
1 Scotch bonnet chile, stemmed,
seeded and minced
6 shallots, thinly sliced
4 cloves garlic, thinly sliced
24 mussels, scrubbed and de-bearded
1 star anise
1 tablespoon freshly ground black pepper
2 cups fresh orange juice
½ teaspoon saffron
1 cup heavy cream
1 cup unsweetened coconut milk
Kosher salt

Six 6- to 7-ounce grouper fillets, trimmed
1 tablespoon pure olive oil
Kosher salt and freshly ground black pepper

Make the sauce: Heat the oil over medium heat in a large, heavy-bottomed saucepan (with a tight-fitting lid on hand). Add the chile pepper, shallots and garlic. Stir and cook for 3 to 4 minutes to let the vegetables soften and flavor the oil.

Add the mussels, star anise and pepper and stir. Add the orange juice and cover the pot. Transfer the mussels as they open to a colander set over a bowl to catch the liquid. (They start opening after about 3 minutes; just take them out as they open, cover the pan again and keep checking for more open ones—about 10 minutes total).

Reduce the orange and mussel juices for about 10 minutes, uncovered, until you have about 1 cup. Add the saffron, heavy cream and coconut milk and bring to a boil over medium-high heat, stirring occasionally (be careful as the cream can boil over). Reduce the cream until it just barely coats the back of a spoon, 5 to 8 minutes. Strain into a bowl, discarding the solids, then strain again through a fine-mesh sieve to remove some of the black pepper flecks. Set aside.

Put the grouper on a large plate and lightly brush both sides with the olive oil. Season on both sides with salt and pepper.

Prepare an outdoor grill for grilling over high heat or heat a large grill pan over high heat. Grill the grouper for 3 to 4 minutes on the first side and 2 to 3 minutes on the second side. You will know it's done when it flakes easily with a fork.

Transfer the fish to warm serving plates and spoon some of the sauce around the fish. (The sauce is quite rich so a little goes a long way). Garnish with tangerine or other citrus sections and serve with cooked asparagus or the best seasonal vegetable.

LITTLE JON'S PORK EMPANADAS FOR A PARTY

We lived on Seidenberg Avenue twice during the 1970s. The first time was a mad period that involved a waterbed in the front yard and a circus-sized tent in the back and all manner of folks coming and going. By the second time, six years later, we were much more settled down—after all, Janet was pregnant. We lived alone in a house that was essentially one room with a small bath in the back and sunlight streaming in from cracks in the walls. Jon's was a short walk away. It boasted "the coldest beer in town," which never failed to impress me—you could reach into the icy waters of a dilapidated, three-legged Coke cooler and drop a full degree of body heat in no time while grabbing a few beers to walk back home, draining one along the way. Jon's also served up some of the standard Key West items found in other little joints in town including pork-stuffed empanadas. Those were likely made by Jon's grandmother and a tad simpler, but less potent, than those I've included here.

Makes about 30 empanadas

FILLING
3½ to 3¾ pounds pork shoulder, cut into 2-ounce pieces
3 tablespoons Escabeche Spice Mix (page 177)
4 red onions, diced
3 carrots, peeled and minced
3 poblano chiles, stemmed, seeded and diced
6 stalks celery, diced
Canola oil, for searing
½ cup pure olive oil or Garlic Oil (page 172)
6 cloves garlic, coarsely chopped
Half 5-ounce can chipotle peppers in adobo, pureed
1 cup red wine vinegar
4 cups coarsely chopped fresh tomatoes
2 cups raisins
4 cups Chicken Stock (page 161)

DOUGH
9 cups all-purpose flour, plus more for dusting
2 tablespoons kosher salt
4 teaspoons baking powder
2 cups vegetable shortening
2 cups ice water, or enough to bind the dough

2 large eggs
Canola oil, for frying

> **Cooking Note:** You can make the filling or dough in advance and store covered or wrapped in plastic wrap in the fridge for a maximum of 2 days.

Preheat the oven to 325°F. Set a roasting pan on the stovetop over high heat.

Make the filling: In a large bowl, toss the pork with the spice mix and set aside.

In another bowl, combine the onions, carrots, poblanos and celery. Set aside.

Once the roasting pan is hot, add enough canola oil to coat the bottom of the pan. Working in as many batches as necessary to avoid overcrowding the pan, sear the pieces of meat on all sides, transferring the pork to a plate once seared.

Lower the heat to medium-high and add the oil. Add the vegetables and cook, stirring often, until they begin to color and soften. Add the garlic and cook until fragrant, about 1 minute. Stir in the chipotle peppers and adobe sauce and cook for 2 to 3 minutes, tossing frequently. Deglaze the pan with the vinegar and reduce.

Transfer the meat to a large Dutch oven. Place the vegetables on top of the meat, then add the tomatoes and raisins. Finally, pour in the stock, cover, and braise in the oven until the meat is fall-apart tender, about 4 hours.

Meanwhile, make the dough: Mix the flour, salt and baking powder in a large bowl. Using a pastry cutter or fork, crumble the shortening into the flour, until the mixture resembles coarse crumbs. Add the water and stir with a fork until the dough forms a ball. Wrap in plastic and refrigerate for 45 minutes. Form the empanadas within 24 hours, as the dough will oxidize quickly.

When the meat pulls apart easily, strain the braising liquid through a fine-mesh strainer into a pot set over medium-high heat and reduce to the point where it will luxuriously coat all the filling with a focused sauce without leaving it soaking wet. Adjust the seasoning, if desired, and chill in an airtight container in the refrigerator for up to ten days, or store in the freezer for up to 3 months.

Spread the meat and vegetables out in the roasting pan to cool slightly, about 10 minutes. Put on a pair of gloves (you can use a potato masher if you don't have gloves) and smash the filling, not to mush, but until it's pretty well busted up. Stir in the sauce and taste.

Before forming the empanadas, whisk together the eggs with some water in a small bowl. Line a sheet pan with parchment paper and dust with flour. Divide the dough into 1-ounce portions. On a well-floured working surface, roll out each portion to ¼-inch thickness. Cut into rounds with a 4-inch cutter.

Place about 1 tablespoon of the filling on each round of dough, brush the edges with the egg wash, and fold the empanada in half. (This might be easier if you pick it up in your hands.) Seal the outer edge with your fingers. Then lay the empanada down on the working surface and crimp the edges with the underside of a fork that has been dipped in flour to prevent it from sticking. Transfer to the prepared sheet pan and lightly dust the empanadas with flour. Continue in batches until all the empanadas are shaped. At

this point, the empanadas can be covered with plastic wrap, then put in a freezer-proof bag and frozen for frying another day, or just refrigerated if frying the same day.

When you're ready to fry the empanadas, preheat a pot of oil to 350°F as measured on a deep-fry thermometer. Fry the empanadas, a few at a time, until nicely golden to golden-brown, about 3 minutes. Transfer to paper towels or a rack to cool for a minute before serving.

FULL MOON FISH SANDWICH

No sandwich in the history of Key West was consumed by more drunks than this one. No sandwich saved more people from a certain lethal-strength hangover. Essentially it is a fresh-as-can-be, Keys-caught fish stuffed in a bun and smothered in cheese and mushrooms. The bar from whence the sandwich was wrought, the Full Moon Saloon, survived the most "party-til-you-drop" years of a very substantial partying town (writers like Jim Harrison and the one and only Hunter S. Thompson made this bar their home away from home when in Key West). The fact that many of the key players who managed and/or owned this saloon survive to this day may be due, in part, to the restorative qualities of the Full Moon Fish Sandwich. Jimmy Buffett wrote "A Pirate Looks at Forty" about one of the most loyal customers, one Phil Clark. His ashes lived over the Full Moon Saloon's cash register for some time. The famed Vietnam war writer Phil Caputo landed the marlin that hung on the back wall of the bar for years. That was until my friend Danny McHugh and I liberated the huge fish and took it back to Danny's home on Riviera, where Danny took pictures of me asleep with said marlin.

Serves 1

Canola or peanut oil, for frying
One 5-ounce grouper (or other fresh fish) fillet, thinly sliced
2 teaspoons fresh lime juice
Kosher salt and freshly ground black pepper
1 large egg, beaten
1 tablespoon buttermilk
1 teaspoon Tabasco or other favorite hot sauce
½ cup beer
4 tablespoons all-purpose flour
4 tablespoons cracker meal or panko breadcrumbs
2 tablespoons unsalted butter
¼ small onion, sliced
4 button mushrooms, sliced
1 hoagie roll (or hamburger bun)
1 to 2 thin slices Cheddar or other favorite cheese
1 pickle, sliced (or pickle slices)
1 ripe tomato, sliced
1 to 2 fresh lettuce leaves, for garnish

Heat 5 to 6 inches of oil in a deep-fryer or deep, heavy-bottomed pot until a deep-frying thermometer registers 350 °F.

Season the fish with the lime juice, salt and pepper.

Combine the egg and buttermilk in one bowl and the beer, flour, and cracker meal in a second one. Dip the fish in the egg wash and then the batter, allowing the fish to soak in the batter a few minutes to help it adhere.

Melt the butter in a pan over medium-high heat and sauté the onion for 4 to 8 minutes, until it begins to caramelize. Add the mushrooms and continue to cook for several minutes, stirring occasionally. Keep warm.

Add the fish to the hot oil and fry for 3 to 4 minutes, until the fish is golden brown and cooked through. (Check by cutting off a small piece.)

Preheat the broiler. Open the roll and toast it briefly under the broiler. Place the fish on the roll, add the mushrooms and onions and top with the cheese. Place under the broiler for about 1 minute to melt the cheese.

Serve with a garnish of pickle, tomato and lettuce or place them directly on the sandwich.

FIVE BROS. BLACK EYE'D PEA BOLLOS

Five Brothers Grocery is just a short walk from one of the Key West Graveyard's iron gates. Since my first voyage to the island, the quiet graveyard remains one of my must visits. The grocery part of Five Brothers is smaller than a one-car garage, but it is stocked with plantain smashers (for tostones*), café con leche makers, paella pans, fishing lures and then some. In addition to this addictive snack, they sell soups and daily specials that include oxtails, chicken fricassee and fresh baked grouper.* Bollos*, or* bollitos*, are a snack from the fritter family, the like of which I never experienced during my childhood growing up in the midwest.*

Makes about 60

12 ounces dried black-eyed peas
1½ teaspoons salt
3 large cloves garlic, minced
2 small Scotch bonnet chiles, stemmed, seeded and minced
½ sweet onion, minced
Canola or peanut oil, for frying

Pick over the peas, discarding any dark ones and debris. Place the peas in a large bowl and cover with water by at least 2 inches. Cover the bowl and let the peas soak overnight.

The next morning, rub the peas between the palms of your hands vigorously to loosen the skins. Remove as much skin as will come off easily, then cover the peas again with cold water and soak for an additional 3 hours; the skins will float to the top. Skim off the skins and rub the peas again to remove any remaining skins. The skins that cling can be lifted off with a thumbnail. (A few remaining skins are all right, but too many make coarse-textured bollitos.)

Using short pulses, grind the peas in a food processor fitted with a steel blade until smooth. Transfer to a large bowl and stir in the salt, garlic, chile peppers and onion. Beat with a mixer or wooden spoon until the batter is thick and creamy then chill thoroughly; the batter can be kept covered in the refrigerator for 1 or 2 days.

In a deep-fat fryer or a large pan fitted with a frying basket, heat 4 to 5 inches of oil until a deep-frying thermometer registers 375°F. Drop the batter from the tip of a teaspoon and fry until golden brown, 3 to 4 minutes. The bollitos should have space to bob around in the oil, so cook in batches, if necessary. Drain on paper towels and keep warm on a foil-lined cookie sheet in a 225°F oven.

These bollos don't require any more accompaniment than a favored beverage.

MOLLETE SANDWICHES

The mollette (moy-EH-tay) sandwich is an entire sandwich that is dipped in egg wash and breadcrumbs before getting the crispy treatment. It is filled with meat, which was crucial for conquering the wobbly constitution I possessed after a night out with one of my sweet lunatic chef buddies back in those line-cooking days. Another specialty of Five Brothers Grocery, this sandwich was the fare I chose to prepare for 800 folks when Emeril Lagasse invited me to join him at the South Beach Wine and Food Festival one year. Many couldn't pronounce it but they sure could enjoy it! Emeril had two.

Makes 4 sandwiches

PICADILLO

4 tablespoons pure olive oil
1¼ pounds ground beef
1 tablespoon unsalted butter
3 cloves garlic, thinly sliced
1 red onion, diced
1 red bell pepper, diced
1 yellow bell pepper, diced
Kosher salt and freshly ground black pepper
1 large tomato, peeled, seeded and coarsely chopped
½ cup tomato paste
1 cup dry red wine
½ cup Sherry wine vinegar
¼ cup chopped small capers, drained and well rinsed
½ cup coarsely chopped raisins or currants
5 tablespoons pitted, lightly rinsed and roughly chopped green olives
¾ cup sliced scallions, mostly white parts

4 short soft sub rolls, hollowed out but still attached on one side (save extra bread for breadcrumbs, if desired)
2 large eggs, beaten with a splash of milk or water
1 cup panko breadcrumbs, or more as needed
Canola oil, for frying

Heat 2 tablespoons oil in a large skillet over medium-high heat. Add the beef and cook until crumbly and lightly browned, chopping the meat up with a spatula, about 5 minutes. Transfer the cooked meat with the juices to a plate and set aside.

Using the same pan, add the remaining 2 tablespoons olive oil and the butter. Add the garlic, onion and bell peppers and season with salt and pepper. Sauté for 10 to 15 minutes over medium-high heat, stirring occasionally, until caramelized.

Add the cooked beef, tomato, tomato paste, red wine, sherry, capers, raisins, olives and scallions; stir and lower the heat to medium-low. Season with salt and pepper and cook for about 15 minutes.

Stuff each sub roll with about a quarter of the picadillo, packing it in tightly to provide a generous amount of filling. Secure the open side of the roll with wet toothpicks. Roll the stuffed sandwiches in the beaten egg and then the panko breadcrumbs until well coated.

Heat the canola oil in a large skillet over medium-high heat and fry each sandwich on all sides until golden and crispy. Remove the toothpicks before serving.

These sandwiches can be prepared 15 to 20 minutes ahead and kept warm in a preheated 300°F oven.

Cooking Note: Here is a perfect example of how your well-stocked Bodega will come to your aid time and again. Before stuffing with the picadillo, take a spoonful of the Red Onion Jam (page 165) and spread it inside the bread, proceed as usual, then, just before digging in to the sandwiches, stuff the openings with some Ice Box Cucumber Pickles (page 168). We often talk about "building flavors" in great cooking—the Bodega items here take mollete sandwiches to new heights.

CRABMEAT ENCHILADOS

I am always researching recipes. It began years ago in Illinois and continued when I was trying to learn my first tangos with Latin and Caribbean cookery. One time at B's, on Bertha Street near Key West High, while enjoying the crabmeat "enchilado," I asked the waitress about the name and she assured me that these were not misspelled Mexican enchiladas but truly spelled with an "o," which has a Spanish origin. Enchilado roughly translates as "with chiles," though you might not find any in the most traditional Cuban versions. Here, I break with tradition and lean toward Haiti, which adds a bit more heat to this dish.

Serves 4 as an appetizer

¼ cup plus 2 tablespoons pure olive oil
3 cloves garlic, thinly sliced
1 habañero or Scotch bonnet chile, stemmed,
seeded and minced
1 sweet onion, diced
½ green bell pepper, minced
1 red bell pepper, minced
1 teaspoon paprika
1 teaspoon ground cumin
Kosher salt and freshly ground black pepper
½ cup chopped fresh cilantro or Italian parsley leaves
1 cup white wine
1 bay leaf, broken
1 cup Chicken Stock (page 161)
One 10-ounce can tomato puree
1 large tomato, peeled, seeded and chopped
½ cup green olives, pitted and finely chopped
1 tablespoon sugar
½ pound crabmeat, cleaned and picked over
Yellow Rice (page 175)

Heat the oil in a heavy saucepan over medium heat. Add the garlic and chile peppers and stir. Add the onion and bell peppers and stir again. Add the paprika and cumin and season with salt and pepper. Stir to release the fragrance of the spices.

Add the cilantro, wine and bay leaf. Reduce for 3 to 4 minutes, until about ½ cup remains.

Add the chicken stock and simmer, stirring occasionally, for about 5 minutes.

Add the tomato puree, tomato and olives and cook over low heat for 10 minutes. Remove from the heat and stir in the sugar.

Add the crabmeat and stir to combine. Heat through—but do not overcook once the delicate crab is added—and serve with rice.

ROPA VIEJA "OLD CLOTHES"

Yes, ropa vieja *means "old clothes" and you might want to be wearing some when you spill some on the front of your shirt while lustily lapping this up. I can imagine a million eyebrows in our large area code go way up when folks read this version of the time-honored dish made with chuck roast rather than skirt or flank steak. I like it just fine made that way, but I love the added richness of the braised chuck and what it does for the sauce. I'm as much of a sauce lover as I am a meat eater and the Van Aken family is all in on this breach with tradition—a potential cardinal sin—and that is a comfort. Serve with the tostones on the next page, rice and any vegetable that won't crush the flavors of the nice red wine you deserve for cooking so well.* **Salud!**

Serves 6

5 pounds 7-bone beef chuck roast, bone in
4 teaspoons Escabeche Spice Rub (page 177)
½ cup pure olive oil
2 tablespoons unsalted butter
2 Spanish onions, thinly sliced
12 cloves garlic, thinly sliced
Kosher salt and freshly ground black pepper
2 cups Beef Stock (page 160)
2 cups water
2 bay leaves
One 28-ounce can peeled plum tomatoes
3 packed tablespoons light brown sugar
1 teaspoon mustard powder
½ cup fresh lemon juice
½ cup Sherry wine vinegar
½ cup ketchup
1½ tablespoons orange zest
8 piquillo peppers, cut into thin strips

Cooking Note:
This is a dish that improves in flavor if made a day or more in advance. Reheat slowly if you make it ahead with a splash of wine, water or beer.

Preheat the oven to 250°F.

Place the chuck roast on a work surface and rub evenly on each side with the Escabeche Spice Rub. Heat half of the oil in a large, heavy saucepan or Dutch oven and sear the meat on all sides over medium-high heat. Transfer to a plate and set aside.

Decrease the heat to medium, add the butter and remaining ¼ cup olive oil to the pan, and when the butter begins to foam, add the onions and garlic and season with salt and pepper. Stir well and cook until caramelized, 8 to 10 minutes.

Deglaze the pan with the beef stock and water, stirring well to lift any meat bits off the bottom of the pan. Decrease the heat to low, add the chuck roast, bay leaves and squeeze in the tomatoes through your fingers into the pan. Bring to a simmer, cover the pan and cook for 2 hours, turning the meat once.

Meanwhile, combine the brown sugar, mustard powder, lemon juice, vinegar, ketchup and orange zest in a small bowl. Cover and set aside.

Once the meat has simmered for 2 hours, add the brown sugar mixture, cover and cook for 1 hour more.

Transfer the meat to a perforated pan with a drip pan underneath to cool. When it is cool enough to handle, shred it along its natural seams and reserve the meat in a clean bowl, discarding the bones.

Meanwhile strain the sauce through a medium-holed strainer into a tall pitcher-like container. Let it settle for about 15 minutes and then skim the fat off the top and discard. Return the sauce to a large, clean saucepan over high heat and reduce the liquid until it reaches about 1 quart. Pour the sauce over the meat, add the piquillo peppers, stir and season with salt and pepper. Stir again and serve.

TOSTONES

The very first exotic ingredient that I fell in love with in Key West during my first trip down was the plantain. The first sweet "kiss" was from the caramelized maduro *ones. (The skins are completely black when ripe enough). Soon after, I had the ones the natives called* tostones, *which is what I make here. Plantains in various forms can be found on plates throughout the Caribbean, whether starchy, crispy, or sweet.*

Serves 6

3 large green plantains (about 1½ pounds)
2 cups canola oil, for frying
Kosher salt and freshly ground black pepper (optional)

With a sharp knife, cut the ends off each plantain and cut a lengthwise slit through the skin. Put the plantains in a deep bowl and cover with very hot water. Let them soak for about 30 minutes.

Remove and peel the plantains and cut them crosswise into 1-inch-thick slices.

Heat a large heavy pot or skillet with 1 inch of oil over medium heat until just hot enough to sizzle when a plantain piece is added. Fry the plantains in batches, without crowding the pot, until tender and golden, about 4 to 5 minutes. Transfer to paper towels to drain. Reserve the hot oil.

While the plantains are still warm, lay a damp kitchen towel on top and smash them fairly firmly with the heel of your hand or the bottom of a heavy saucepan to make ¼-inch-thick slices. (At this point, you can keep them wrapped in the damp towel for up to 2 hours until ready to fry.)

Heat the reserved oil over medium heat until hot but not smoking and fry the flattened plantains in batches, without crowding the pot, until golden brown, about 2 minutes.

Transfer the tostones to paper towels to drain and season with salt and pepper if desired. Serve immediately.

CHULETAS EMPANIZADAS

This dish is another one so good that it impelled me to learn more Spanish. When translated into English, you will see these are simply breaded and fried pork chops. But the flavor is more than that! The truck stop–sized Chuletas Empanizadas at El Siboney in the neighborhood near Catherine Street where we lived while working at the Pier House (called La Lechonera back then), inspired me to finesse this dish to make a more manageable portion yet with all of the powerful flavors intact. I didn't get the exact recipe nor did I try—I offer this as my rendition, based on my memory, as an homage. We like to serve this with our Black Beans (page 163), Yellow Rice (page 175) and Mango Chutney (page 166).

Serves 4

Four 10-ounce pork chops
2 very ripe plantains, sliced ½-inch thick
Kosher salt and freshly ground black pepper
Peanut or canola oil, for frying
4 tablespoons unsalted butter
½ cup all-purpose flour
1 tablespoon Escabeche Spice Rub (page 177)
2 large eggs, beaten
2 tablespoons milk
2 cups breadcrumbs

Cut a pocket in each pork chop by laying them on their sides and making a lateral cut in each one toward the bone. Set aside.

Season the plantains with salt and pepper. Heat a sauté pan over medium-high heat until just hot. Add ½ inch of oil and fry the plantain slices until they are quite dark on all sides. Transfer to a plate and dab them with paper towels. Let cool for a few minutes, then place the plantains in a shallow bowl and mash with the butter. Season with salt and pepper and set aside.

Spoon 4 to 5 tablespoons of the plantain stuffing in the center of each pork chop (any leftover mashed plantain can be saved for another use). Reshape the pork chops, pressing them back together around the stuffing.

Preheat the oven to 400°F.

Place the flour in a shallow bowl and stir in the Escabeche Spice Rub. Mix the eggs and milk together in another shallow bowl. Place the breadcrumbs in a third shallow bowl. Dredge the chops in the flour, then dip them in the eggs, allowing the egg wash to soak in a minute. Finally, press the chops in the breadcrumbs to coat.

Heat a large, heavy-bottomed sauté pan over medium-high heat until hot. Add enough oil to coat the bottom of the pan and add the pork. Sear the chops on both sides for about 2 minutes total. Remove any excess oil from the pan and place it in the oven for 15 to 20 minutes, or until a instant-read thermometer inserted horizontally into a chop reads 145°F.

Transfer the pork to a cutting board to rest in a warm place for about 5 minutes before serving.

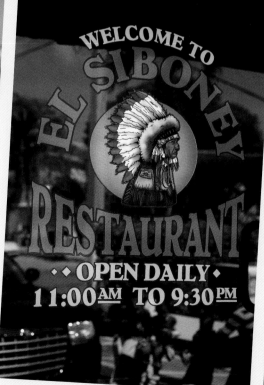

WELCOME TO
EL SIBONEY
RESTAURANT
◆◆ OPEN DAILY ◆
11:00 AM TO 9:30 PM

PLACES ON THE WATER

It is instructive to remember that there are not many places in the entire U.S. of A. that are not reachable via automobile. It is rather astonishing to note that Key West far out-populated Miami for decades, despite the fact a citizenry could not arrive there to settle it (and even prosper) except via an ocean. The Overseas Highway system changed that slowly in the 1940s. When we motored over the skinny (and seemingly swaying!) bridges in the 70s, we got our first look at the Island. Hemingway arrived via boat 40 years ahead of us—as did many of the artists that came here and co-created a culture that endures.

1978 TO 1979: THE PIER HOUSE

Make no mistake about it, the Pier House was an important contribution to the city of Key West and its economic future. When the navy pulled out of Key West in the mid-1970s, the economy cracked. The tourist industry was dormant, and when David Wolkowsky turned a one-time fish market at the end of Duval Street into the low-key but elegant resort, the Pier House, it marked a change in the opportunity for well-to-do northerners to camp out in style in our island town. It also became a haven for the well-moneyed gay population that began to visit and then buy homes in Key West in droves. Times were changing once again in Key West, and David was a giant in the turning tides.

When I got a job as a breakfast cook at the Pier House I was, once again, the lowest man on the totem pole. But it turned out to be worth it; I was finally in a place where I could learn. David Wolkowsky was a visionary man who loved many kinds of flavors. He installed chefs who were early adapters to what became known as New American Cuisine. A small but vital group had just graduated from the Culinary Institute of America in Hyde Park, New York. Somehow, David had the instinct

to know that this youthful energy allied with a few older hands from Europe, was exactly the right formula to enchant the artists from New York City to come play, drink and eat at the Pier House. By the time I got there, guests like Leonard Bernstein and Truman Capote were already tasting the Pier House's Conch Chowder, Yellowtail Snapper and Key Lime Pie.

But I was an unknown to any of them at that point. I cooked under a watchful, sometimes wrathful, always chattering woman named Betty Howard. She was my boss, my scolder, my savior. Betty taught me some dishes, tricks and moves that are still with me to this day. Annie Donovan was the head chef, and when I graduated to the night shift she took me under her wing, showing me dishes out of her CIA cookbooks. When I asked her for the requisite letter of recommendation to attend a cooking school, she stopped me and said, "I'll make you sous chef. I'll teach you what you would learn there. You won't have to pay tuition. Just bust your ass for me." I'll always be grateful to her for doing that. Between Annie and Betty, I went from being a no-nothing line cook to one who was starting to look for more in life than a hot line.

Chef-patron Philip Mascia
of the Port of Call

1979: THE PORT OF CALL

If there was one restaurant that finally made me want to succeed at becoming a serious chef it was the Port of Call. I'd been cooking for over eight years and I'd been with clowns, cowboys and ruined chefs enough. I had heard about the mercurial Philip Mascia, his talent and his restaurant's popularity. The place was packed every night with the very height of Key West's in-crowd, a mini version of New York's Le Cirque or Elaine's. Philip was the "chef-patron"—what some of the chefs in France called themselves. The idea of being one myself one day began to wave its hand in front of my mind's eye and say, "It's now or never, Buddy Boy."

We did it all there. There wasn't a prep or butcher department, saucier, *entremetier, poissonier, commis* or any of the other Frenchy terms I was starting to hear and feel less than smart about. We received the fish in the alley behind the kitchen and cut it right there before we put it in the reach-in cooler. We had a household refrigerator in a back closet behind the dirty linen bags. It wasn't fancy but it was functional. Still, there was an artisan's atelier feeling to the kitchen at Port of Call. The tools were all carefully chosen. It was the first time I had seen professional-grade saucepans for almost every sauce. Unlike the other places where I worked, this was not a hodgepodge of battered cookware. It was almost like entering a Williams-Sonoma store except the Port of Call tools bore the patina of being proud use.

1987: THE CAFÉ AT LOUIE'S BACKYARD

The inspiration for the Café came from a visit to San Francisco I took with Proal Perry in the spring of 1987. We were knocked completely out by places like Stars, Square One, Fog City Diner and Chez Panisse. It was while we sat in the Café at Chez Panisse that we realized we could transform the upstairs of Louie's into our version of Alice Water's revolutionary, yet informal, Berkeley mecca. Our concept featured one of the first "small plate" menus in America. We wanted to distinguish the café from the traditional format of the menu at Louie's Backyard one story below and we also wanted a way to be less conventional. It worked.

K.W.I. CONCH FRITTERS

When you fly into Key West, the Spanish words Bienvenidos a Cayo Hueso! *greet you upon arrival, signaling that you ain't in America so much anymore! Key West's airport is called Key West International, and back in the 1970s, the airport was more like a funky bus terminal in a southern town with a bar called the Great Escape that featured an all-girl topless band. It was owned by Stacy Harnish and the menu offered various preparations with the clam-like mollusk known as conch. We locals loved it. These days you can buy them from Venda Storr, pictured at right, who has taken up frying and selling perfect conch fritters from the convenience of her driveway*

Makes about 3 dozen

2 large eggs
½ cup whole milk
1¼ cups all-purpose flour
¼ cup baking powder
1 teaspoon kosher salt, plus more for seasoning
½ teaspoon freshly cracked black pepper
1 tablespoon Roasted Garlic (page 172), mashed,
or ½ tablespoon minced raw garlic
2 tablespoons minced sweet onion
1 tablespoon seeded and minced jalapeño pepper
2 tablespoons minced red pepper
½ cup beer
4 squirts Tabasco sauce, plus more for seasoning
1 pound cleaned conch meat, freshly ground
Canola or peanut oil, for frying
Lemon and/or lime wedges, for garnish
Cocktail Sauce (page 164)

In a medium bowl, beat the egg, then stir in the milk.

In a large bowl, sift together the flour, baking powder, 1 teaspoon salt and pepper. Add the egg mix to the flour mix and stir to combine.

Stir in the garlic, onion, japapeño and red pepper, then the beer and Tabasco. Fold in the conch and chill the batter in the refrigerator, covered, for at least 30 minutes or overnight.

Heat 2 inches of oil in a deep fryer or large pot until a deep-frying thermometer registers 350°F.

Using two spoons or a small ice-cream scoop, carefully add small balls of fritter batter, about 1 tablespoon each, into the hot oil. Cook, turning the fritters over from time to time, for about 5 minutes—their color when done will vary with the quality of the oil. Transfer to paper towels to drain.

Season the fritters with salt and Tabasco. Serve hot with the lemon and/or lime wedges and cocktail sauce on the side.

Ingredient Note: You can grind conch yourself as you would beef for hamburgers, or ask your fishmonger to do so. If conch is not available where you live, the fritter batter is also quite capable of hosting finely chopped lobster, clams or shrimp.

SUNSET CELEBRATION

Before more than two nights elapse in any visit to Key West you will be guided to take in the Sunset Celebration at Mallory Square. It was love at first sight for us when we first took in the scene. Imagine people from all walks of life just coming together to marvel at the sun's graceful descent into the Gulf of Mexico. Nothing jaded. Nothing for sale about it. Just life being observed and celebrated. It had the carney elements to be sure and still does. Sword swallowers, the ageless tightrope walker Will Soto, jugglers, cat trainers, fortune tellers, dope dealers I knew and didn't, food sellers (the Cookie Lady, the Banana Bread Man and so on) and the rest of us—hippies, straights, gays, shopkeepers, navy guys, tourists. My friend Steve and I would often hurl ourselves into the water and race to the first buoy and back while the sun did its thing. The illuminated faces of "the congregation" still shines in my memory and on the Mallory Dock each evening.

Serves 1

1¼ ounces Bacardi light rum
½ ounce Triple Sec
½ ounce amaretto
2 ounces fresh orange juice
2 ounces fresh pineapple juice
1 ounce fresh grapefruit juice
1 ounce Angostura grenadine
Pineapple, orange and lime slices for garnish

Mix all of the ingredients except the fruit garnish in a cocktail shaker. Fill a pint glass halfway with ice cubes and pour the drink over the ice. Garnish with pineapple, orange and lime slices.

Ingredient Note: Go to a juice bar and get fresh pineapple juice for this or juice one if you can. The taste is incomparable.

"90 MILES TO CUBA" RUM RUNNER

The mayor of Key West in the late 1970s, Sonny McCoy, was a character worthy of a Hollywood bit part, if not a starring role. From the "only in Key West" annals, he actually water-skied to Cuba in September 1978. I imagine he cut out from the Southernmost Point where the land-based buoy still colorfully displays the sign "Only 90 miles to Cuba!" It took him just three and a half hours. Amazing. Enough so that I'm going to drink to that: Here is our "90 Miles to Cuba" Rum Runner, a tribute to Mayor McCoy.

Serves 1

1 ounce fresh pineapple juice
1 ounce fresh orange juice
1 ounce blackberry liqueur
1 ounce banana liqueur
1 ounce light rum
1 ounce dark rum or aged rum
Splash Angostura grenadine
1 ounce Bacardi 151, for floating on top (optional)
Orange slice, for garnish (optional)

Mix all of the ingredients except the optional Bacardi and orange slice in a cocktail shaker. Fill a pint glass halfway with ice cubes and pour the drink over the ice. Add a splash of Bacardi to float and garnish with the orange slice, if desired.

WHOLE ROASTED SNAPPER
WITH ANCHOVY BUTTER

Philip Mascia, the chef-owner of the Port of Call was also a young father and he decided to throw a birthday party for his little girl, Sohmer, at the Sands, which was situated at the end of Simonton Street right on the ocean. Philip was an incredible natural chef. Back then, I thought you pretty much only knew the food that you cooked on your menu but when it came to this party, Philip unveiled a very beautiful whole snapper he had baked on the grill wrapped in aluminum foil and festooned with herbs and lemons. He offered it with the Port's much-requested anchovy butter.

Serves 2

One 2-pound whole snapper, gutted and scaled
Kosher salt and freshly ground black pepper
½ cup white wine
3 tablespoons extra-virgin olive oil
4 to 5 fresh thyme sprigs
2 to 3 bay leaves
1 lemon, sliced
1 medium red onion, sliced
1 small bulb fennel, cored and sliced

ANCHOVY BUTTER

½ cup (1 stick) unsalted butter, softened at room temperature for at least 30 minutes
6 anchovy fillets packed in olive oil, rinsed well and chopped into a near paste
1 teaspoon freshly ground black pepper
1 tablespoon strained fresh lemon juice

Preheat the oven to 400°F.

In a large pan, place a piece of aluminum foil large enough to wrap the fish. Place the fish on the aluminum foil. With a sharp knife, make slashes in the flesh 1 to 1½ inches apart, almost to the bones. Season the fish with salt and pepper on both sides and pour the wine around the it. Drizzle some of the olive oil on the fish and the rest into the wine. Scatter the thyme and bay leaves around the fish and add a few lemon slices (save the rest for garnish), the onion and fennel. Fold up the foil and seal the edges to create a packet. Roast the packet of fish in the pan for 30 to 35 minutes, or until cooked through.

Meanwhile, make the Anchovy Butter: In a serving bowl, combine the softened butter, anchovies, pepper and lemon juice; mash together thoroughly with the back of a fork.

Unwrap the fish at the table and serve with the Anchovy Butter on the side.

Ingredient Note: I prefer to use anchovies labeled "Wild Caught." The Anchovy Butter yields about ¼ pound. You can store it in a sealed plastic container or rolled up like a cigar in plastic wrap.

Cooking Note: Cooking times can vary significantly, but the fish can be kept warm and retain its moisture for a long time if it's kept wrapped in the foil.

A COOLER FULL OF SANGRIA

While at his child's birthday party, Philip pulled out a trick I'll never forget: He filled an office-sized water cooler with homemade sangria and plugged it in under the grass-thatched roof of the tiki bar. The lemons, limes and oranges bobbed happily in the red wine. I like to use Evodia "Old Vine" Grenache red wine for this sangria, which tastes better the next day.

Makes 1 gallon, about 10 to 12 servings

2 oranges
2 lemons
2 limes
1 pineapple
2 large mangoes
½ cup sugar
½ cup lemon juice
Four 750ml bottles Spanish red wine,
preferably Grenache
12 ounces fresh orange juice
10 ounces brandy
8 ounces curaçao
12 ounces club soda

Cut the citrus fruits into 6 wedges each, rind and all. Skin the pineapple and cut into pieces roughly the size of one of the citrus wedges. Peel, pit and chop the mango into pieces about the same as the other fruit.

In a small bowl, stir the sugar and lemon juice until the sugar is completely dissolved. Put the sweetened lemon juice with the rest of the ingredients, except the club soda, into a large dispenser and chill in the refrigerator to allow the flavors to marry. Chill the bottle of club soda as well.

Once the mixture is adequately chilled, add the club soda to the rest of the sangria. Serve over ice.

BAHAMIAN CONCH CHOWDER

When Janet had just turned 21, she got a job waitressing at a joint that had served Key West for eons. Justifiably named the Fisherman's Café, it was a working-class place a short walk from the docks. By seven A.M., the shrimpers were sitting elbow by tattooed elbow at the counter where she delivered eggs, sandwiches, beers and their Bahamian conch chowder. Here is my take on that.

Serves 12

4 ounces slab bacon, trimmed and diced
½ cup pure olive oil
6 cloves garlic, sliced
1 jalapeño pepper, seeded, stemmed and diced
2 Scotch bonnet chiles, seeded, stemmed and minced
1 large Spanish onion, diced
8 celery stalks, diced
2 carrots, diced
1 bulb fennel, diced
1 red pepper, diced
1 yellow pepper, diced
1 tablespoon crushed red pepper flakes
1 quart peeled plum tomatoes, thoroughly crushed
1 quart tomato puree
3 bay leaves, broken
2 tablespoons chopped fresh basil
4 cups Chicken Stock (page 161)
2¾ quarts bottled clam juice
2½ pounds cleaned and ground conch meat
1 pound Baby Red Bliss Potatoes, scrubbed and diced
Tabasco, for seasoning

In a very large soup pot or Dutch oven, cook the bacon in the olive oil until the fat is rendered. Add the garlic, both kinds of chile peppers, followed by all the vegetables. Sauté over medium-high heat until just beginning to soften. Stir in the crushed red pepper flakes.

Add the tomatoes and tomato puree, being sure the plum tomatoes are well crushed. Reduce the heat to a simmer and stir in the bay leaves and chopped herbs.

In another large pot, bring the chicken stock and clam juice to a boil. Gradually whisk in the ground conch. Return to a boil over medium-high heat and quickly strain the liquid into the simmering soup, reserving the conch meat. Let the soup simmer to concentrate the flavors slightly, about 5 minutes longer.

Add the diced potatoes and simmer until tender, about 15 minutes. Stir in the reserved conch meat and add Tabasco to taste. Bring to a boil over medium-high heat and serve hot.

Cooking Note: This chowder can be made ahead and refrigerated in an airtight container for up to 3 days.

DAVID'S BAKED POTATO SKINS
WITH MUSTARD AND BÉARNAISE

Real estate developer and owner of the Pier House, David Wolkowsky is a visionary who had a great deal to do with the restoration of Key West. His eccentricities were also celebrated widely on the Rock. It was not uncommon for him to "set a table" in the kitchen of the Pier House: To David, this meant placing a sheet pan with some napkins on top of an empty upside-down garbage can so he could watch our kitchen hum during service. One night he asked us for a potato-skin snack. He loved the dish we came up with and they became "the usual." These baked potato skins are vegetarian, but you could add steamed shrimp or a slice of shredded ham on top.

Serves 4

TARRAGON REDUCTION
½ cup red wine
½ cup red wine or tarragon vinegar
¼ cup diced shallots
1 teaspoon freshly ground black pepper
½ cup finely chopped fresh tarragon leaves
1 tablespoon chopped chervil (optional)

6 baked potatoes
1 tablespoon Dijon mustard

BÉARNAISE SAUCE
1 cup (2 sticks) unsalted butter
3 egg yolks
1 tablespoon Tarragon Reduction, or to taste
1 tablespoon fresh lemon juice, or to taste
Tabasco sauce, to taste
Kosher salt

> Cooking Note: The Tarragon Reduction can be made ahead of time but it is important to bring it to a warm room temperature before using it in the Béarnaise.

Preheat the oven to 400°F.

Make the Tarragon Reduction: In a small heavy-bottomed saucepan, combine the red wine, vinegar, shallots, pepper, tarragon and chervil, if using. Reduce over medium-high heat until all of the liquid is evaporated, about 20 minutes. Set aside.

Wrap the potatoes in foil, prick with a fork and bake until the skins are fairly crisp, 60 to 70 minutes.

Meanwhile, make the Béarnaise Sauce: Cut the butter into several pieces and melt it over low heat in a skillet. Over medium heat, heat a pot of water that will hold a stainless-steel bowl without letting the bowl come into contact with the water. Put the egg yolks in the bowl, add just a few drops of water and whisk vigorously with a balloon whisk. Add 1 tablespoon, or more to taste, of the tarragon reduction and whisk very well.

Place the bowl in the pot over the simmering water and whisk—do not stir—the egg yolks, letting them thicken gently and evenly. You can adjust the heat, and thus the speed at which they cook, simply by lifting and lowering the bowl. You do not want the eggs to cook too quickly or they will not be as velvety. When you can draw a line with the whisk across the bottom of the bowl and see the bottom for a quick count to three, the eggs are ready. Continue whisking once the bowl comes off the heat, but do not allow the mixture to cool.

Remove the bowl from the heat and gradually beat in the melted butter. When it is all incorporated, whisk in the lemon juice and Tabasco. Taste and add more of the tarragon reduction if needed. Season with salt and keep warm.

Working quickly, place the warm potatoes on a work surface. Cut them in half lengthwise and scoop out the potato's interior (which can be saved for another use). Brush some mustard on the inside of each potato "boat" and cut them into tortilla-chip shapes. Return the skins to the oven to recrisp, about 5 minutes. Top the hot potato skins with some of the warm Béarnaise sauce and serve.

BLACK BETTY'S PAN-COOKED YELLOWTAIL

This is the way I was taught to cook this wildly popular recipe by a woman who lived in the Bahama Village section of Key West. She was the breakfast chef at The Pier House and her name was Betty Howard. We offered it pan-cooked and served whole on the bone with lemon butter and parsley potatoes. Yellowtail is in the snapper family and it is possibly the mildest, most tender, sweetest snapper of them all. In the old days of Key West, the fishmongers would load up their bicycle baskets with yellowtail and roll along the little lanes in the early morning hours selling the fish to housewives who would cook it for breakfast. It may seem odd to many to have fish for breakfast, but that's how mild and sweet it is. If you can't find yellowtail snapper, any other thin, delicate fish will do.

Serves 4

2 eggs, beaten
½ cup half and half
Kosher salt and freshly ground black pepper
Four 7- to 8-ounce yellowtail snapper fillets
½ cup all-purpose flour
¼ cup Clarified Butter (page 180)
1 lemon, cut into wedges

Preheat the oven to 400°F.

In a large mixing bowl, beat the eggs with the half and half and salt and pepper. Set aside.

Season the fish fillets with salt and pepper on both sides, then dust with the flour and shake off any excess. Put the fish into the egg wash and leave them there up to 2 hours, until ready to cook.

Heat a large sauté pan over medium-high heat. When the sauté pan is hot, carefully ladle in the clarified butter. Lift the fish out of the egg wash with one hand and gently lay the fish into the hot butter, using both. Gently shake the pan and cook for about 2 minutes. When the first side is deeply golden, turn the fish over with a spatula, tilting the butter toward the bottom of the pan and flipping the fish toward the top to avoid splashing, and cook for another 1 to 2 minutes.

Drain off all the excess butter into a catch bowl and bake the fish in the oven for 7 to 10 minutes (the thickness of the fish will determine the cooking time), or until it flakes easily with a fork.

Serve immediately with wedges of lemon on the side.

> **Cooking Note:** The sweet flavor of clarified butter is part of the reason this dish is so beloved. Of course you can substitute a less rich source of fat. Just don't look for Betty's approval if you do.

G.D.F. CAKE (A CHOCOLATE LAYER CAKE)

For the full, uncensored story of how this cake got its name, you can read my memoir No Experience Necessary *where it is revealed! But for the purposes of this cookbook, let's just say G.D.F. stands for glorious, delicious and fantastic! This recipe is a bit labor-intensive because you are essentially making two types of cake and marrying them. In the end, you will have a cake that looks like it belongs on the cover of a magazine and tastes like it could win at the county fair to share with your family and friends. Enjoy with a cold glass of milk or a neat glass of fine island rum.*

Serves 10 to 12

CHOCOLATE CAKE

4 cups granulated sugar
3½ cups all-purpose flour
1½ cups cocoa powder
1 tablespoon baking powder
1 tablespoon baking soda
2 teaspoons kosher salt
4 large eggs, at room temperature
1 cup whole milk
1 cup sour cream
1 cup canola oil
2 tablespoons pure vanilla extract
2 cups hot coffee

COCONUT CAKE

1¼ cups cake flour, plus more for the pans, sifted
½ teaspoon baking soda
½ teaspoon kosher salt
½ cup (1 stick) unsalted butter, at room temperature, plus more for the pans
1 cup granulated sugar
3 large eggs, slightly beaten
½ tablespoon pure vanilla extract
½ cup buttermilk
1 cup flaked unsweetened coconut

Preheat the oven to 315°F with the rack in the middle. Butter and lightly flour four 10-inch round cake pans.

Make the chocolate cake: Sift all of the dry ingredients into a large bowl; mix and set aside. In the bowl of a stand mixer, whisk together the eggs, milk, sour cream, oil and vanilla. Add the dry ingredients and, using the paddle attachment, beat until the batter is smooth with no lumps. Add the coffee slowly, scraping the bowl thoroughly between each addition. (This will be a very loose batter.)

Divide the chocolate cake batter between two of the prepared cake pans and bake for 35 to 40 minutes, or until a toothpick inserted into the center of the cakes comes out clean. Cool slightly in the pans, then invert gently onto wire racks to cool completely. (The cakes will be very delicate.) Refrigerate until ready to assemble.

Make the coconut cake: In a small bowl, whisk together the flour, baking soda and salt and set aside. Cream the butter and sugar in the bowl of a stand mixer fitted with the paddle attachment until pale and light. Add the eggs, a little at a time, stopping and scraping down the sides of the bowl and paddle once with a rubber spatula, and beat until white and fluffy. Add the vanilla extract and a quarter of the buttermilk and blend until smooth. Stir in the dry ingredients and blend until the batter is smooth with no lumps, stopping and scraping once. Slowly add the remaining buttermilk, stopping and scraping once. Gently stir in the flaked coconut.

Divide the coconut cake batter between the remaining two prepared cake pans and smooth with a spatula. Tap the sides with a wooden spoon to dispel any air bubbles. Bake for 35 to 45 minutes, or until a toothpick inserted into the center of the cakes comes out clean. Cool in the pans for about 15 minutes, then invert onto wire racks to cool completely. Refrigerate until thoroughly chilled.

Meanwhile, make the ganache: In a small saucepan over medium-high heat, bring the heavy cream and espresso grounds just to a boil. Set a fine-mesh strainer over a heatproof bowl filled with the chocolate pieces and pour the hot cream mixture over the chocolate.

GANACHE

1 quart heavy cream
1½ tablespoons espresso grounds
1½ pounds semisweet dark chocolate (about 54% cocoa), cut up into small pieces
1 tablespoon coffee extract

COCONUT-PECAN FILLING

1 cup evaporated milk
1 cup granulated sugar
½ cup light brown sugar
½ cup (1 stick) unsalted butter
1 teaspoon pure vanilla extract
1⅓ cups unsweetened coconut flakes
1 cup chopped pecans

Let sit for about 1 minute, until the chocolate softens, then stir in the coffee extract until well combined. Cool completely at room temperature until thickened, at least 2 hours or overnight.

About 30 minutes before assembling the cake, make the filling: In a small saucepan, combine the evaporated milk, both sugars, and butter and cook over medium heat, stirring, until thickened, about 12 minutes. Stir in the vanilla, coconut and pecans. Cool the filling until thick enough to spread. (It should still be slightly warm.)

Assemble the cake: Place one layer chocolate cake, rounded side up, on a cake plate. With an offset spatula, spread half of the coconut-pecan filling over the layer. Top with a layer of coconut cake, rounded side down, and spread a quarter of the ganache on top. Repeat with layers of chocolate cake, the remaining half of the filling, another quarter of the ganache and the coconut cake, rounded side down. Frost the assembled cake with the remaining ganache and refrigerate overnight before serving.

PORK HAVANA, KEY WEST STYLE

We made this the first Christmas I worked at the Pier House. I felt quite far away from my midwestern home, celebrating a holiday usually marked with steady snowfall, glowing fireplaces and a great, fragrant roasted prime rib of beef on a long table at my grandmother's house. But in our tropical kitchen at the end of Duval Street we also felt we were uniting with different cultures—and the spirit of Christmas should accomplish that every year. Waiter Tom Goetz brought in a bottle of rum and we made punch. By the end of service, we were singing Christmas carols as we cleaned up the kitchen. Home was near again. I like to serve this with Cayo Hueso Cornbread (page 20), Yellow Rice (page 175) and Black Beans (page 163).

Serves 4

2 sour oranges, cut in half
2 oranges, cut in half
4 limes, cut in half
½ cup pure olive oil, plus more for searing
8 whole black peppercorns, bruised
2 bay leaves, broken
6 cloves garlic, thinly sliced, plus 3 cloves, peeled and cut into studs
½ red onion, thinly sliced
One 4-bone rack of pork (about 3½ to 4 pounds)
Kosher salt and freshly ground black pepper
5 to 6 bacon strips

GLAZE

1 tablespoon pure olive oil
1 tablespoon unsalted butter
3 cloves garlic, thinly sliced
1 sweet onion, finely chopped
Kosher salt and freshly ground black pepper
1 orange, cut in half
1 tablespoon freshly toasted and ground cumin seeds
1½ tablespoons sherry wine vinegar
¼ cup orange marmalade

Ingredient Notes: A four-bone rack of pork is like four pork chops but still attached. Ask for one at your butcher's shop. If you can't find sour oranges, use regular ones but add 2 tablespoons of cider vinegar when squeezing the juice into the marinade bowl.

Squeeze the juice of the orange and lime halves into a large bowl then toss in the rinds as well. Add the oil, peppercorns, bay leaves, sliced garlic and red onion and stir to combine. Place the pork in the marinade, turn the rack a few times to coat evenly, and marinate in the fridge for up to 24 hours, but at least 8 hours, turning it a few times.

Remove the pork from the marinade and gently scrape off any oil and other bits. Pat dry with paper towels. Using a sharp knife, puncture the pork all over and push the garlic studs into the holes. (The holes can be a bit bigger than the studs, so the marmalade mixture to come can seep into the pork as it cooks.) Slash the pork with a crosshatch pattern and season all over with salt and pepper.

Preheat the oven to 375°F.

Make the glaze: Heat a heavy saucepan over medium heat. Add the oil and butter and swirl to melt. Add the garlic and onion, lower the heat to medium and cook slowly and steadily until caramelized, seasoning with salt and pepper and adding the cumin about halfway through.

Chop one of the orange halves into small pieces. Squeeze the juice of the other orange half through a fine-mesh strainer (to catch the seeds) into the saucepan. Toss in the chopped orange, rind and all. Add the vinegar and reduce by a third. Stir in the orange marmalade and heat until melted. Transfer the glaze to a small bowl and let cool slightly.

Heat oil in a large heavy skillet over medium heat. Sear the pork on all sides until browned, about 10 minutes. Transfer to a plate and let cool.

Spoon the glaze onto the pork, letting it seep into the punctures. Lay the bacon strips on top, overlapping slightly. Wrap the top of the pork roast securely with aluminum foil to keep the bacon from falling off.

Roast the pork in the oven for 45 minutes. Carefully remove the foil and roast for another 35 to 40 minutes, or until the pork reaches an internal temperature of 145°F on a meat thermometer.

Transfer to a cutting board and let the roast rest for at least 10 minutes before carving.

SPINACH SALAD
WITH PIQUANT DRESSING, BASIL, SPICED PECANS & BLUE CHEESE

My first job at the Port of Call was on the salad line. We didn't have prewashed salad greens in those days and there was so much grit, you might have thought the spinach came from the beach. I dumped a barrel's worth of spinach in a deep prep sink and filled it with cold water. The sand fell to the bottom and I shook the leaves out with violence until it passed the "chew test" the chef had instructed me to follow. Philip's lessons were simple but they stuck: "I better not get any #@^*ing sand in my mouth." Dipping my arms in the cold sink full of water was the only good thing about the chore. But the salad was delicious and very popular. I have added a few elements since to the original recipe, but the piquant dressing is the same.

Serves 4 to 6

PIQUANT DRESSING
2 cups ketchup
2 cups pure olive oil
1 cup red wine vinegar
½ cup tarragon vinegar
½ cup extra-virgin olive oil
1 tablespoon kosher salt
1 tablespoon Dijon or Creole mustard
1 tablespoon freshly ground black pepper
½ tablespoon paprika
½ sweet Vidalia onion, diced
6 hard-boiled eggs, chopped

SPICED PECANS
1 teaspoon cayenne pepper
1 teaspoon crushed red pepper flakes
1 teaspoon hot paprika
1 teaspoon chile molido) or pure red chile powder
1½ teaspoons kosher salt
¼ cup sugar
1 large egg white
¼ cup sorghum (or maple) syrup
1 pound raw pecan halves

SPINACH SALAD
6 cups spinach leaves, washed and stems trimmed
1 cup fresh basil leaves
½ cup blue cheese, crumbled
1 cup croutons

Preheat the oven to 315°F.

Make the dressing: In a medium bowl, whisk together all of the dressing ingredients except the eggs. Fold in the eggs and set aside. You'll have more than enough for this salad so save some in the refrigerator for another day.

Make the spiced pecans: In a small bowl, whisk together all the dry ingredients for the spiced pecans in a bowl. In a large bowl, whisk the egg white and maple syrup to loosen the egg white. Toss the pecans in the mixture. Add the dry ingredients and toss until all of the pecans are evenly coated.

Spread the pecans out on a sheet pan and roast them, stirring and turning intermittently, until toasted and somewhat dry, 20 to 25 minutes. Let cool for 1 to 2 hours, until they become crunchy.

Make the spinach salad: In a large bowl, toss the spinach leaves with the dressing, as desired. Toss with the spiced pecans, basil, blue cheese and croutons and serve.

Ingredient Note: Look for Maytag blue cheese out of Iowa or Asher Blue from Sweet Grass Dairy in Thomasville, Georgia. They are not salty and appeal to a broad range of tastes.

PORT OF CALL CRAB & AVOCADO SALAD

Everything I learned about cooking was ramped up in the little Port of Call kitchen. Making things to order was one of the obsessions I picked up there. We made beurre blanc to order in Philip's kitchen, which was a far cry from the 3 or 4 pounds of batches we kept at the ready at the Pier House. At first, it was intimidating to cook on the edge like that, but then it made us proud. This stuffed avocado recipe from the Port of Call redefined the concept of salad for me, which before always meant a bowl of lettuce. Once again the Port of Call changed my levels. Back then we made them with the Mexican Hass avocado variety and since they are small we would stuff all of the goods back in the avocado shell. Now I use the larger Florida avocados when in season and we don't serve it stuffed.

Serves 4

2 avocados, cut in half, pit discarded
Kosher salt
1 cup blue crabmeat, drained if wet, and loosely broken up into bite-sized pieces
¼ cup diced celery stalks, inner hearts
1 tablespoon chopped fresh Italian parsley leaves
2 teaspoons stone-ground or Creole mustard
4 cups fresh mixed greens
¼ cup Champagne Vinaigrette (page 166), plus more for garnish
1 tablespoon finely grated Parmesan (optional)

Remove the flesh from the 4 avocado halves and dice it into medium pieces. Sprinkle with a bit of kosher salt.

In a large bowl, combine the avocado, crab, celery, parsley, mustard and greens, taking care to be gentle with the avocado and crab. Toss with the Pineapple Sesame Vinaigrette. Refrigerate before serving, but not more than 10 minutes.

Garnish with the Parmesan, if desired, and serve.

Ingredient Notes: If you are lucky enough to find Florida avocados, you'll only need one for this salad. At the Port we finished this salad with Parmesan but let your imagination and seasonality guide yours.

GRILLED DUCK BREASTS
WITH RAISIN-PINEAPPLE SAUCE

The sauce in this dish is a descendant of Cumberland, a sweet fruit-based concoction I first glimpsed in The Professional Chef Cookbook, *the companion to the Culinary Institute of America's educational curriculum. I hung out with grads from that vaunted school in my Pier House days. I never could swing the tuition, but that didn't stop me from borrowing the cookbook. I began to make a version of the sauce with chiles and spices to give it more buzz. In this recipe, the allure comes from luscious tropical fruit, always welcome with duck. It is also amazing with ham and pork, but fine for chicken as well. The sauce makes 2 ½ cups, so you may have some left over.*

Serves 4

2 double duck breasts, cut in half and trimmed
Extra-virgin olive oil, for coating
Kosher salt and freshly ground black pepper
Champagne Vinaigrette (page 166)
4 cups frisée lettuce

RAISIN-PINEAPPLE SAUCE
2 cups diced pineapple
1 cup red wine vinegar
1 cup light brown sugar
½ cup seedless raisins
1 cup currant jelly
2 tablespoons orange marmalade
2 tablespoons fresh lime juice
1 teaspoon lime zest
½ teaspoon ground cinnamon
½ teaspoon ground cloves
½ cup Chicken Stock (page 161)

Ingredients Note: At the Port of Call, we served Long Island duckling but that was before gourmet purveyors like Ariane Daguin offered D'Artagnan. I did this recipe with their superb Magret de Canard.

Make the sauce: In a medium bowl, combine all of the ingredients for raisin-pineapple sauce and mix well. Transfer to a heavy saucepan and cook over medium heat until syrupy. Keep warm.

Score the skin of the duck breasts in a crosshatch pattern almost down to the meat. Season with salt and pepper and lightly rub with oil.

Preheat the oven to 350°F.

Heat an outdoor grill to medium hot, or set a grill pan over medium-high heat. Rub the grates or pan with a little oil to prevent sticking. Grill the duck breasts, turning often to reduce any flare ups from the skin, for 4 to 5 minutes. Transfer to the oven and cook until the meat is medium-rare, about 7 minutes, or until a meat thermometer inserted into the thickest part of the thigh registers 125°F. Transfer to a cutting board, tent with aluminum foil, and let rest before slicing.

In a large bowl, toss the frisee with the vinaigrette. Season with salt and pepper if desired.

Spoon the raisin-pineapple sauce onto four plates. Thinly and evenly slice the duck breasts crosswise. Season with a little more salt and, using a spatula or knife, gently place the duck on top of the sauce. Mound the salad alongside or on top of the duck and serve.

MY HOT FRIED CHICKEN SALAD

I received the biggest break of my career to date when I became Executive Chef of Louie's Backyard in June 1985. When developing the menu, one of the owners demanded that I keep a steak salad from the previous chef. It was a big seller to be sure, but I was not going to have some other chef's dish on my menu. So I presented my Hot Fried Chicken Salad the next night. More than 17 years later, I moved on but this Hot Fried-Chicken Salad was still on the menu. The dressing and marinade each make 2 cups, so you may have some left over.

Serves 4

HONEY MUSTARD DRESSING
2 egg yolks
1 tablespoon honey
¼ cup Creole mustard
1 cup canola oil
⅓ cup extra-virgin olive oil
2 tablespoons dark roasted sesame oil
¼ cup sherry wine vinegar (or balsamic vinegar)
1 tablespoon Sriracha
Fresh lemon juice to taste
Kosher salt and freshly ground black pepper

HOT FRY FLOUR
1½ cups all-purpose flour
¾ tablespoon kosher salt
2 tablespoons freshly ground black pepper
3 tablespoons crushed red pepper flakes
¾ tablespoon cayenne pepper

MARINADE
3 large eggs, beaten
1 cup heavy cream
¾ tablespoon paprika
1 jalapeño pepper, stemmed, seeded and thinly sliced
¾ tablespoon crushed red pepper flakes
¾ tablespoon cayenne pepper
Kosher salt and freshly ground pepper

4 boneless chicken breasts, sliced widthwise into "finger" shapes (skinless optional)
Peanut oil for frying
1 to 2 heads inner romaine leaves, torn or chopped into bite-sized pieces
¼ to ½ red onion, thinly sliced into rings

First, make the dressing: Beat the egg yolks in an electric mixer with the honey and mustard until pale. Gradually add in the three oils, with the machine still running. (If the dressing gets too thick add a little vinegar). Finish adding the oils and then the remaining vinegar. Add the Sriracha. Season with lemon juice, salt and pepper. Set aside.

Mix together all of the ingredients for the Hot Fry Flour. Keep it in a sealed container until ready to use.

Next, make the marinade: In a large bowl, beat the eggs with the cream. Add the paprika, jalapeño, crushed red pepper and cayenne and mix well. Season with salt and pepper. Add the chicken and stir to coat all the pieces. Cover with plastic wrap and marinate for at least 4 hours, preferably overnight.

When ready to cook, remove the chicken fingers from the marinade and roll them in the flour mixture to coat thoroughly.

Heat a large sauté pan over medium-high heat. Add enough peanut oil to immerse the chicken. When the oil is hot enough, carefully lay some of the chicken fingers in the hot oil. Working in batches as necessary to avoid crowding the pan, fry until golden brown on one side, then turn them over and fry until brown on the other side. Transfer to paper towels to drain, and keep warm. Clean out the pan between batches.

Put the romaine leaves in a large bowl, add enough dressing to coat and toss. Divide the dressed leaves among four serving bowls. Cut the fried chicken into bite-size pieces and sprinkle on top of the greens. Add the red onion rings and serve immediately.

CARAMEL FLAN CON COCO

I had a flan con coco *at a Cuban roadside place in Marathon, one of the major keys of the island chain that dot the ocean, as I was hitching out of town a long time ago. I wanted a last taste of the place I was falling in love with to take with me.*

Makes about 12 individual flans
or 1 family-sized flan

1 cup sugar
One 12-ounces can evaporated milk
One 13.5-ounce can unsweetened coconut milk
One 14-ounce can sweetened condensed milk
3 large eggs
3 egg yolks
½ tablespoon pure vanilla extract
1 teaspoon kosher salt
1 cup sweetened shredded coconut

Cooking Note: Caramelizing
half of the sugar, then adding
the rich combination of milks
creates a flavor reminiscent
of another beloved confection
from Latin American cooking—
dulce de leche.

Preheat the oven to 275°F. Make sure the canned milks are open as you'll need to add them quickly when the caramel is done.

To make the caramel, combine ½ cup sugar and a little water (just enough to form a wet sand) in a saucepan over medium-high heat. Melt the sugar, stirring often, until there are no more lumps. (Note: If any sugar touches the sides of the pan, be sure to wash all the crystals down into the sugar mixture with clean water and a pastry brush before the mixture comes to a full boil.)

When the caramel reaches a deep amber color, turn off the heat. Carefully stir the milks in the order listed; the mixture will bubble and hiss. Transfer to a blender, then add the eggs, egg yolks, vanilla, and salt and blend until smooth. Set aside at room temperature for 30 minutes or more, allowing the custard to rest and deflate.

Meanwhile, prepare the baking dishes: Scatter the shredded coconut in the bottom of each baking dish. Set the baking dishes in a large baking pan and pour in enough very hot water to reach halfway up the sides of the dishes.

Divide the custard evenly among the baking dishes. Cover with aluminum foil and bake until set, 30 to 40 minutes for the smaller ones or 45 minutes to 1 hour for one large flan. To test for doneness, gently shake the baking pan: If the flans jiggle like a just-set Jell-O, take them out of the oven or they will become overdone. If the liquid is still sloshing around a bit, give them more time.

Once the flans are done, remove them from the water bath and let come to room temperature. Cover and refrigerate overnight before serving.

SHRIMP PO' BOY WITH HOT SAUCE VINAIGRETTE

When Janet took a second job bartending at the Half Shell Raw Bar, the shrimp boats were still part of the scene. I always loved to have the Shrimp Po' Boy and a very cold bottle of beer that Janet had wrapped a napkin around like she learned from Roby up at the Top. Garnishes on the sandwich are really up to you: Top with Ice Box Pickles (page 170), barbecue sauce, or crumble some of your favorite potato chips over the shrimp, then close the bun and enjoy!

Makes 1 sandwich

SHRIMP
2½ cups canola oil
½ cup all-purpose flour
2 tablespoons Escabeche Spice Rub (page 177)
1 large egg
2 tablespoons water
½ cup cornmeal
3 medium to large shrimp, peeled and deveined

One 10- to 12-inch-long piece of French bread
4 tablespoons mayonnaise
3 tablespoons Creole mustard
Pickle slices (optional)
1 cup shredded lettuce
1 tomato, sliced or chopped (optional)
Hot sauce (optional)

In a large heavy-bottomed pot, heat the oil until a deep-frying thermometer registers 360°F.

In shallow bowl, season the flour with 1 tablespoon of the Escabeche Spice Rub. In another shallow bowl, whisk the egg with the water until well combined. In a third bowl, mix the masa harina and cornmeal and the remaining 1 tablespoon spice rub.

Dredge the shrimp in the seasoned flour, then the egg wash, then the corn flour mixture to cook. Fry the shrimp until just golden brown, 2 to 3 minutes. If doubling the recipe, do not overcrowd the pan, and let the oil come back to 360°F before adding another batch. Transfer the fried shrimp to paper towels to drain.

Slice the bread lengthwise about three-quarters of the way through, leaving it hinged. Spread the mayonnaise on the bottom half. Spread the mustard on the top half. Arrange the pickles and tomato, if using, on the bottom half and fill the po' boy with lettuce. Top with the fried shrimp and serve with your favorite hot sauce on the side.

Ingredient Note: I have had shrimp from all over and those out of Key West and the Gulf of Mexico are the very best. They are sold frozen more often than not. Just defrost them in the refrigerator overnight and resist doing it in the sink as it washes out the shrimp's sweet flavor.

SWEET POTATO CAKES
WITH CAYENNE & BLACK OLIVE TAPENADE

The menu at the Café was an early innovator of the small-plate revolution that soon swept America and remains to this day. We sought to create big flavors even if in smaller venues. This dish is sweet, salty, spicy and savory all with just a few ingredients. It is a perfect snack for cocktail hour to fortify the gang for Duval crawlin' later.

Serves 4 to 6

BLACK OLIVE TAPENADE
¼ cup milk
2 anchovy fillets, drained and rinsed
1½ cups black Mediterranean-type olives, pitted and chopped
4 tablespoons capers, drained and rinsed
2 tablespoons fresh lemon juice
1 teaspoon Dijon mustard
Freshly ground black pepper
4 tablespoons cognac
¾ cup pure olive oil

SWEET POTATO CAKES
1¼ pound unpeeled sweet potatoes, scrubbed
1¼ pound unpeeled boniatos, scrubbed
4 tablespoons unsalted butter
1 large onion, chopped
1 small bunch scallions, diced
4 tablespoons Roasted Garlic (page 172)
3 tablespoons chopped fresh basil leaves
1 teaspoon chopped fresh cilantro
1 teaspoon chopped fresh thyme leaves
2 egg yolks
Kosher salt
Cayenne pepper, for seasoning
Peanut oil, for frying

Make the tapenade: Soak the anchovies in milk for 30 minutes. Drain and rinse again. Blend all of the tapenade ingredients except the oil. Whisk in the oil. This makes about 2 cups.

Put the sweet potatoes and boniato in a large pot, cover with cold water and bring to a high simmer. Cook until almost but not quite done. Drain well and chill, uncovered, for at least 3 hours.

Heat a large heavy skillet over medium heat and melt the butter. Sauté the onion, scallions and garlic, stirring, for 3 to 5 minutes. Drain the excess liquid from the vegetables. Add the fresh herbs, cool slightly and transfer to a large bowl. Stir in the egg yolks, salt and cayenne.

Peel the boniato and shred them along with the potato on the large holes of a box grater. Add to the vegetable and herb mixture, stirring to combine. Taste for seasoning.

Preheat the oven to 375°F. Form the sweet potato mixture into cakes about 2 inches in diameter and 1 inch thick. Set aside on a baking sheet until ready to cook.

Heat a skillet over medium-high heat. Add enough peanut oil to coat the bottom of the pan. When the oil is hot, add the cakes without crowding. Cook, turning over once, until browned on both sides, then place the cakes in the oven for 8 to 10 minutes to heat through.

Transfer the sweet potato cakes to individual plates, top each with Tapenade and serve.

> **Storage Note:** Leftover tapenade is excellent on toasts with soft cheeses. It will keep for weeks in the refrigerator if covered with a light film of extra-virgin olive oil and refrigerated.

WILD MUSHROOMS ON BRIOCHE
WITH SHERRY CREAM & SERRANO HAM

Serrano ham was not widely known outside of New York City in the United States when I put this appetizer on the menu at the Café at Louie's Backyard. If you can't find Serrano ham, prosciutto works well too. Use whatever good quality mushrooms are in season. This dish would be very good paired with perfectly ripe tomatoes or Garlic Oil Roasted Potatoes (page 172). Or if fruit is what you want, offer sweet melon or beautiful strawberries splashed with aged sherry wine vinegar. Or perhaps, as an homage to Alice Waters, a mesclun salad with just a hint of your favorite dressing.

Serves 4

3 tablespoons extra-virgin olive oil
2 cloves garlic, thinly sliced
¾ pound wild mushrooms, trimmed and cut into quarters or sixths
Kosher salt and freshly ground black pepper
1 tablespoon unsalted butter
3 tablespoons sherry wine vinegar
¾ cup heavy cream
4 slices brioche
4 very thin slices Serrano ham
Fresh Parmesan, for garnish

Heat a large sauté pan over medium heat then add the olive oil. Add the garlic and cook for 1 minute to soften. Add the mushrooms and stir gently. Season with salt and pepper and sauté for about 3 minutes, until cooked through. Add the butter and stir to combine. Add the vinegar and simmer for 30 to 60 seconds.

Transfer the mushrooms to a strainer set over a bowl to allow the natural liquids to drip through. Press down to get every last drop then return the liquid to the sauté pan. Keep the mushrooms warm.

Turn up the heat to high and reduce the liquids in the sauté pan until almost syrupy. Add the heavy cream and reduce the sherry mixture until thick enough to coat the back of a spoon.

Return the warm mushrooms to the cream mixture and keep warm.

Toast the brioche and place on four plates. Top with the mushroom mixture and lay a slice or two of Serrano ham over each serving. Grate some Parmesan on top and serve.

HONEY MANGO ICE CREAM
WITH MACADAMIA NUT COOKIES

This recipe unites three of our favorite places. I ran off to Hawaii when I was 19 and soon became passionate about the local Hawaiian food, especially macadamias. When I got to Key West two years later, mangos were in abundance and mercifully still are—we have three varieties growing in our yard. Lastly there is a place we shop whenever we pass through Florida City. It is an amped-up fruit and vegetable stand named Robert is Here. Robert has been there for generations and we find his honeys, which come in about 20 different flavors, irresistible.

Makes 1 quart

MANGO ICE CREAM
3 cups mango puree
Juice of 1 lemon
1 cup heavy cream
⅓ cup honey
⅔ cup granulated sugar
9 large egg yolks
Pinch kosher salt

MACADAMIA NUT COOKIES
Makes 30 cookies
2½ cups all-purpose flour
1 teaspoon baking powder
½ teaspoon kosher salt
6 tablespoons unsalted butter
½ cup granulated sugar
½ cup light brown sugar
1 large egg
¼ cup honey
½ teaspoon pure vanilla extract
2½ ounces toasted (salted is fine) macadamia nuts, chopped medium-fine
2 ounces good-quality white chocolate chips, chopped fine

Make the ice cream: In a pot over medium heat, combine the mango puree, lemon juice and cream. When the mixture is hot, stir in the honey and 5 tablespoons of the sugar. In a medium bowl, whisk the egg yolks with the remaining 5 tablespoons sugar until pale.

When the mango mixture just begins to scald, turn off the heat and stir some of it into the yolks to gently raise their temperature. Once the yolk mixture is hot, add it to the pot, stir and return to a low heat.

Cook, stirring frequently, until the mixture thickens enough to coat the back of a spoon or registers 180°F on a candy thermometer. Remove from the heat, stir in the salt, strain through a fine-mesh sieve and chill fully before churning according to manufacturer's instructions.

Make the cookies: In a large bowl, whisk together the flour, baking powder and salt. In the bowl of an electric mixer, cream the butter and both sugars well. Lower the speed and add the egg, then the honey and vanilla extract. Turn off the mixer, scrape down the beater and the sides of the bowl with a rubber spatula and beat until fluffy.

Stir in the flour mixture, just to incorporate. Stir in the nuts. Turn over the dough onto a large piece of parchment paper, form into a log, 2 inches in diameter, and refrigerate until well chilled, at least 4 hours or overnight.

When ready to bake the cookies, preheat the oven to 325°F. With a sharp knife, cut the log of cookie dough into ⅜-inch-thick slices to make 30 cookies in all. Arrange on two cookie sheets and bake until just done, about 15 minutes. Cool for 1 minute on the sheets, then transfer to a wire rack to cool completely.

Serve bowls of the mango ice cream with a handful of macadamia nut cookies on the side.

AROUND TOWN THESE DAYS

Justin (JVA): My own personal connection with Key West "just comes natural, like the first breath from a baby." I was brought into this world at Florida Keys Memorial Hospital in May of 1980, and as an infant of only a few months, I watched hundreds of people reach American shores from Cuba during the Mariel boat lift. Not that I understood the historical and cultural significance of what I was watching—nor would I realize, before returning to Key West at twenty-one years of age, that I had also already experienced my first Fantasy Fest, possibly from the same stroller. But I did know, upon leaving Key West for Boca Raton at age nine, that I was leaving my home—a unique, beautiful and peaceful world unto itself, and that we were moving to what seemed like a very large and mysterious "mainland," as we Conchs refer to the rest of the contiguous United States.

In 2007, while living once again in Key West, my dad and I began to cook together a lot. He taught me things I hadn't yet mastered, like butchering chicken, sauce making, and meat cookery (we really like to grill steaks when we're at home). I became much more personally invested in food and cooking than I ever had been before and would pester him with constant questions: Why do you do this? Why not that? How do you know this . . . ?

The following year, I moved to Chicago, where I became enchanted with the farm-to-table ethos, which brought me out to the San Francisco Bay area in the fall of 2009 to investigate it further. In between, I pressed a copy of Barbara Kingsolver's *Animal, Vegetable, Miracle* and Michael Pollan's *Omnivore's Dilemma* into my father's hands. As he read, we talked; we discussed our loftier goals and the "real and lasting legacy" of our family business.

It turned out that our restaurants had (albeit in a somewhat unfocused way) supported local farmers and artisans over the years. This came naturally to my father, who was raised in farm country himself. We both agreed that to "eat locally, think globally" meant something very special to us and that doing so in South Florida and the Florida Keys would be a very unique challenge for us indeed.

In this chapter, we show you around the island; not as we remember it, but as we find it today. These days we cook at home for most meals. But we do, of course, sometimes prefer to have someone else chop the vegetables and do the dishes, so we'll head down to one of a few local spots that are reliably putting out good seafood, sandwiches, snacks or cocktails. Eating out around town inspires us continually, adding new dishes to our repertoire, keeping us both well-fed, and still somehow hungry for more.

NORMAN (NVA)

This chapter reflects how I cook "these days." The lead up for me was 40 years of kitchen hot lines: you can develop a really complicated cooking style when you go that route. But the funny thing is, you also get it out of your system (if you want to). Today I draw on all of the techniques I've learned over the years, but I also know how to pull the one gun I need instead of the whole militia. It is relaxing.

I started cooking because I needed a job—gainful employment, rent money, food money, "taking a girl named Janet out" money—but the amazing feeling of cooking is what keeps me completely and passionately involved in it each day. I dream of food. I awake from my own personal "night kitchen" many mornings.

OUR KEY WEST CUISINE

The other place I stumble out of dreams into is the most "South of the Souths" in our U.S. of A. It is a place laying in an ocean in the humid and equatorial extremes. It is where I drink my iced café con leche out of a Mason Jar on a hot spring morning and ponder the unity between the lost remnants of Dixie and the estranged ones of Cuba. Each still creates the two dominant chords of my version of Key West cuisine. I am from the North and so I am neither Southern nor Cuban but I like to consider myself a "multitude"—whether it's bourbon one night or Havana Club rum on another is anybody's guess. Language differences may seem to divide us, but the DNA between the American South and the islands of the Caribbean is much the same in the kitchen, on the porches, in the churches, and at the boatyards of Key West. We are in the clasp of different cultures but slightly askew, afloat here in the Gulfstream off Florida. Yet the spirit of Key West is in the fish my son and I both prize, the lard melting in cast-iron pans, the sweet fruits that hang heavy from our trees, the beans we simmer, the greens we treasure. Even I don't know what will next compel me to

make a little magic, as the great Colette liked to call cooking. I can still amble down Windsor Lane, the very first street I knew in this old town, and smell the blooming night flowers, listen to the song of palm leaves amidst the complaint of a cat, graze against the slanted walls of what is now called Charlie's Grocery (La Farola long ago), and tiptoe past the graveyard. This path gives me a measure of calm few places on Earth ever have. Why do I love this island so much? The answer is blowing in the Gulf winds. Come see for yourself, and give these favorite recipes of ours a try.

I'm lucky to call Key West a home and—by the time you read these words—I'm likely to be making grand-baby food for the youngest in our clan. I hope to make it the best food yet.

FORBIDDEN FRUIT COCKTAIL

NVA: Almost every fruit cocktail is a concoction that overstates fruit's inherent sweetness. It almost seemed to me that to offer a more savory version was forbidden. Naturally, that inspired me to do exactly that! If you don't have mamey available, use any other ripe fruit of your choice. The vinaigrette is excellent for finishing grilled pork ribs, marinating a fatty fish for the grill or a hot wok or as used here—a dressing for luxurious fresh fruits!

Serves 4

1 cup diced ripe pineapple
1 cup diced ripe mango
1 cup diced ripe mamey (or other ripe fruit)
½ cup fresh (or dried) figs, stems discarded

SPICED PINEAPPLE-SOY-VANILLA VINAIGRETTE
1 ripe pineapple, trimmed, cored, and cut into pieces
1 cup fresh orange juice
1 jalapeño pepper, stemmed, seeded and minced
1 to 2 Scotch bonnet chiles, stemmed, seeded and minced
2 tablespoons minced fresh ginger
1 vanilla bean, split in half lengthwise
2 tablespoons apple cider (or white wine) vinegar
1 cup extra-virgin olive oil
2 tablespoons tamari or light soy sauce
Squeeze or more of fresh lime juice
Kosher salt and freshly cracked black pepper

Prepare all the fruits and set aside in the refrigerator.

Make the vinaigrette: Place the pineapple and orange juice in a blender and pulse until smooth. This makes about 5 cups.

Transfer to a saucepan and add the jalapeño, 1 of the Scotch bonnets, 1 tablespoon of the ginger and the vanilla bean. Reduce over medium-high heat until you reach about 2 cups. Remove from the heat and let steep for 15 minutes.

Strain the pineapple puree through a fine-mesh sieve into a large bowl; you should have about 1 cup. If you have more than 1¼ cups, reduce the puree again until you have 1 cup.

Add the remaining 1 tablespoon ginger, the vinegar, oil, tamari, another ½ to 1 chile, if desired, lime juice, salt and pepper to taste and whisk well. Gently fold in the fruits and chill until serving.

STONE CRAB GAZPACHO

NVA: What soup could be more perfect in the late afternoon of a hot day to fuel a young cook, enabling him to take on a night of serving a hundred hungry diners? When working at the Port of Call, I went through a phase that bordered on mania quaffing down this soup, sometimes known as "liquid salad," in shocking quantities. The recipe is descended from the ancient Romans so originally it could not have involved tomatoes. But Columbus changed that and, to my belly, all for the better. It is one of the few soups that contains vinegar. Buy a high quality one and the flavors of the soup will shine. And, of course, the addition of stone crab makes this your Sunday best.

Serves 4 to 6

4 large ripe tomatoes, peeled, seeded and coarsely chopped
½ red onion, diced
1 yellow bell pepper, diced
1 European (hothouse) cucumber, peeled, seeded and diced
¼ cup extra-virgin olive oil
3 cloves garlic, minced
¼ cup plus 2 tablespoons red wine vinegar
2 cups tomato juice
½ teaspoon freshly toasted and ground cumin
A few dashes Tabasco sauce
Kosher salt and freshly ground black pepper
1½ cups cubed bread, toasted or sautéed in olive oil until golden brown
2 cups cleaned stone crabmeat or other crabmeat

In a large bowl, combine all of the ingredients, except the croutons and crabmeat, cover, and refrigerate until thoroughly chilled, 2 to 3 hours.

Working in batches, if necessary, place the chilled soup in a blender and quickly but very briefly pulse the soup. Gazpacho is best when it retains some nice texture.

When ready to serve, taste to adjust the seasonings; you may need some salt. Ladle into chilled soup bowls, top with the croutons and crab and serve.

Ingredient Note: We prefer a variety of heirloom tomatoes that have almost no seeds and are brilliant red. You will get superior results if you can make this during the peak tomato season.

CHILLED CORN, CURRY & SPINY LOBSTER SOUP

NVA: The old timers in the Keys still call spiny lobster "crawfish." Too often when you have a guest eat the kind of lobster native to our waters they express a bit of chagrin in that it is not as buttery-tasting as the claw-bearing variety that Maine is so well known for. I mostly think of the spiny creatures as big shrimp and almost nobody minds that notion! This soup is also beautiful garnished with thinly sliced apple and more cooked corn kernels. JVA: When my dad wrote the "Fusion" paper, he was originally referring to a marriage between "haute" and "home"; the cuisine of monarchs with the food "that mama used to make." If you look closely, you can see that this dish is the love child of an exotic curried lobster with all the homey comfort of a side of creamed corn.

Serves 6

3 tablespoons unsalted butter
2 leeks, white part only, diced
2 tablespoons curry powder
4 cups fresh corn kernels, cut off the cobs (about 4 ears)
1½ cups apple juice
3 cups Chicken Stock (page 161)
Bouquet garni of ¼ teaspoon coriander seeds, 5 black peppercorns and 6 stems cilantro with leaves, tied in cheesecloth
1½ cups heavy cream
1 cup unsweetened coconut milk
2 squirts of Tabasco sauce (optional)
Kosher salt and freshly ground black pepper
1 to 1½ cups of half and half
Sour cream, for garnish

SPINY LOBSTER

2 pounds spiny lobster meat (or shrimp), shelled and cut into bite-sized pieces
¼ cup plus 2 tablespoons pure olive oil
Kosher salt and freshly ground black pepper

Melt the butter in a medium pot over medium heat. Add the leeks, cover, and sweat until soft but not browned, about 5 minutes.

Add the curry and cook, stirring, for 1 minute. Add the apple juice and reduce by three-quarters. Add the corn, chicken stock and bouquet garni. Simmer uncovered for 20 minutes.

Add ½ cup of the heavy cream. Stir and remove the pot from the heat. Add the coconut milk and set aside for 30 minutes for flavors to steep.

Remove and discard the bouquet garni. In batches, purée the soup in a blender, or alternatively use a stick blender. Stir in the remaining 1 cup heavy cream and the Tabasco, is using. Strain through a large-holed sieve into a medium bowl. Season with salt and pepper and chill thoroughly in the refrigerator. (The soup may be very thick at this point.) Stir in the half-and-half to a desired consistency and set aside.

Meanwhile, make the spiny lobster: Heat a nonstick sauté pan and heat the oil. Add the lobster meat and cook over low heat until cooked through. Transfer to a plate and set aside to cool.

Add the cooled lobster to the soup and taste to adjust the seasoning. Garnish with sour cream to taste, and serve.

Cooking Note: Spiny lobster is tough if not cooked somewhat slowly and completely through. If you want a lighter hue to the lobster, simply steam the tails and then cut them up and add to the soup. The cooking juices from the lobster can be saved to drizzle over grilled fish or spoon into a shrimp stir-fry with rice.

Ingredient Notes: Though corn seems to be available year round these days, I like to make this soup during the absolute height of sweet corn season. Look at buying spices like you would buying fish or meat—and the likelihood is that your spices will be with you for weeks or months to come, so get the best!

GULF SHRIMP & SPINACH SOUP

NVA: Lunchtime at home often finds me tinkering in the kitchen in search of a tasty midday meal. This often means tossing things into a soup of sorts. Don't think for a minute that I make "whatever 'n' water soup"! Many surprisingly heroic soups have just sort of happened using this approach. Perfect examples include this Gulf Shrimp and Spinach Soup or the preceding Grilled Corn, Curry and Spiny Lobster Soup. This one is very nice served with a lightly toasted baguette.

Serves 4

4 tablespoons pure olive oil
4 tablespoons unsalted butter
6 cloves garlic, thinly sliced
1 poblano chile, stemmed, seeded and diced
½ red onion, diced
1 pound shrimp, peeled and deveined, chopped into bite-size pieces
Kosher salt and freshly ground black pepper
1 cup white wine
2 cups Chicken Stock (page 161)
1 pound baby spinach, preferably organic, stemmed and chopped
1 cup heavy cream

Heat a large heavy soup pot over medium heat and add the oil and butter. When the butter is melted, add the garlic, poblano and red onion and cook for 7 to 8 minutes, stirring.

Add the shrimp and cook through, 4 to 5 minutes. Season with salt and pepper. Add the white wine and stir. Transfer the shrimp to a bowl.

Reduce the liquid in the pot by half. Add the chicken stock and reduce until you reach 2 cups.

Stir in the spinach leaves and cook for 5 minutes. Stir in the heavy cream and reduce by about a quarter. Return the cooked shrimp to the pot and season with salt and pepper to taste.

Transfer the soup to a blender and pulse briefly. Ladle the soup into four warm bowls and serve.

CATFISH WITH LEMON BBQ SAUCE

NVA: This dish reaches to Texas, thanks to my guitar pickin' and soulful singin' chef-pal Dean Fearing, who walked me straight through the back door of the famed Sonny Bryan's Barbeque temple when on a trip to Dallas, stuck a spoon into Sonny's sauce pot and let me taste some heaven. Between that sauce and crispy-sweet catfish, I started thinking of a having Southern wedding on the plane ride back to Key West.

Serves 4

Four 8-ounce boneless, skinless catfish fillets
Kosher salt and freshly ground black pepper
1 large egg, beaten
¾ cup buttermilk
1 cup yellow cornmeal
½ cup all-purpose flour
Peanut or canola oil, for frying
Java Gal's Lemon BBQ Sauce (page 167), for serving

Preheat the oven to 400°F.

Lightly season the catfish fillets with salt and pepper.

In a shallow bowl, whisk together the egg and buttermilk. Mix together the cornmeal and flour in another shallow bowl.

Dip the fillets into the egg wash, then coat liberally with the flour mixture and set aside.

Over medium heat, heat a skillet large enough to hold the fillets without crowding (or work in batches). Add enough peanut or canola oil to generously coat the pan. When the oil is hot, lay the fillets in the skillet, curved side down, and gently shake the pan. Cook until the fillets are golden on one side, about 2 minutes, then flip them over. Remove any excess fat from the pan and bake in the oven for about 3 minutes, or until cooked through.

Transfer the catfish to a platter lined with paper towels to drain for a few minutes. Arrange on warm plates and serve with the lemon BBQ sauce on the side.

MANGO BBQ'D-GRILLED SWORDFISH

NVA: Mangoes originated in India, but today they are loved in cuisines all over the world. The Sanskrit word for mango is amra, *meaning "of the people." I think barbecue means "of the people" in America so I have united them here. Justin and I demonstrate this dish at mango festivals from time to time. The bonus: We always bring a bowl of it premade so that the guests can have a taste. That means the batch we make up on stage comes home. You'll be left with half of the BBQ sauce from this recipe, but you'll be pleased as you can use it on any kind of thing in the world that you might barbecue. It is outrageously good on a burger.*

Serves 4, plus leftover BBQ sauce

MANGO BARBECUE SAUCE
2 tablespoons pure olive oil
½ large red onion, chopped
1 clove garlic, minced
¼ cup fresh orange juice
1 tablespoon ground black pepper
½ cup white wine vinegar
1 tablespoon dark brown sugar
½ tablespoon Hungarian hot paprika
One 14-ounce can peeled plum tomatoes, chopped
1½ cups diced ripe mango
2 tablespoons sugar
¼ cup Creole or Dijon mustard
¼ cup molasses
1 teaspoon chili powder
2 tablespoons soy sauce
1 tablespoon Worcestershire sauce
¼ cup chopped fresh basil
½ tablespoon freshly toasted and
ground cumin seeds

Four 7- to 8-ounce swordfish steaks, trimmed
Scant 2 cups Mango BBQ Sauce
1 mango, peeled and sliced, for garnish

Heat a large heavy saucepan over medium heat, add the oil and onion and stir. Then let the onions caramelize, without stirring.

Add the garlic and stir for about 1 minute. Add all of the remaining BBQ sauce ingredients, bring to a boil, then reduce the heat and simmer for 50 to 60 minutes, stirring occasionally, until you have a little over 3 cups sauce. Leave chunky or puree in a blender or food processor. Set aside to cool.

Remove the swordfish steaks from the refrigerator and let sit for 30 minutes at room temperature before cooking them.

Prepare an outdoor grill for grilling over medium-high heat or preheat a grill pan over medium-high heat. Grill the swordfish steaks for 3 to 4 minutes on the first side and 2 to 3 minutes on the second side, until browned on the outside and cooked through.

Transfer to warm serving plates and spoon some of the mango BBQ sauce around the fish.

"PEEL 'N' EAT" PINKS

NVA: By the time happy hour rolls around, I try to find myself a seat at the bar at Hogfish Bar and Grill, located on the shrimp docks of Stock Island (just outside of Key West) for a cold brew and an order of "Peel 'n' Eat" Pinks, served up by the inimitable Ms. Patty Whacker. Bobby and Michelle, the owners, might join us and offer up whatever fish came in that day. This dish is always best eaten outside staring at a relentlessly beautiful expanse of the Gulf of Mexico (it also goes well with a chilled cocktail or white wine). It is simple, a tad messy and so satisfying that it may as well be the edible emblem for knowing how to live right. JVA: Leftover "Peel 'n' Eats" are great for pastas, soups, stir frys, omelettes, shrimp dip, or even condiments and spreads with the help of your food processor. Don't skimp on the shrimp!

Serves 6 to 8

1 tablespoon allspice berries
½ tablespoon black peppercorns
½ tablespoon mustard seed
1 teaspoon whole cloves
1 tablespoon pure olive oil
1 teaspoon fennel seeds [when is this added?]
½ red onion, coarsely chopped
6 cloves garlic, cut in half
2 bay leaves, broken
4 bottles beer
1 lemon, cut in quarters
36 large shrimp (about 2½ pounds), preferably Key West Pink, still in their shells
Cocktail Sauce (page 164)

Heat a large saucepan over medium-high heat. Add the allspice, peppercorns, mustard seed, and cloves and toast for about 30 seconds. Add the olive oil and when hot add the onion, garlic and bay leaves. Stir and cook until the vegetables are translucent. Add the beer, squeeze the juice from the lemon quarters into the pot, then throw them in. When the beer comes to a boil, add the shrimp.

When the liquid returns to a boil, the shrimp should be done. Strain the shrimp in a colander then chill over ice.

When ready to serve, place the cocktail sauce in a bowl in the center of the table and arrange the shrimp in bowls, with or without ice around them. Provide an empty bowl or dish on the table for the guests to discard the shells.

CONCH & GRITS WITH SALSA ROSA

NVA: Time and time again, eating in town and strolling the quiet lanes of Key West awakens my imagination. One morning after I'd had my breakfast grits, I couldn't pass up a fresh batch of cracked conch from the Conch Shop on Petronia, where Shorty has been dipping conch in a fryer for most of his 86 years in Key West. The light crispy batter and fresh, slightly chewy conch meat made me wish I had them with my grits! I've enjoyed shrimp and grits throughout the South, especially in Charleston, SC, but I wanted to pay homage to the mollusk that Key Westers are nicknamed for in another way besides chowder and fritters (both of which we've included in this book). So, I married a Charlestonian idea to a Key West one and sealed the union with fiery Salsa Rosa. I also like to serve this piquant sauce with fried calamari. If you like your food less spicy, cut down on or omit the crushed red pepper.

Serves 4

SALSA ROSA

½ cup minced slab bacon, rind trimmed and discarded
¼ cup pure olive oil
2 tablespoons unsalted butter
4 cloves garlic, thinly sliced
3 shallots, thinly sliced
⅓ cup sugar
1 tablespoon crushed red pepper flakes
½ cup red wine vinegar
2 cups Chicken Stock (page 161)
6 tomatoes, peeled and roughly chopped (about 3 cups)
Kosher salt and freshly ground black pepper
⅓ cup thinly sliced fresh basil leaves

CONCH

1½ pounds conch meat, cleaned and pounded very thinly
Kosher salt and freshly ground black pepper
2 tablespoons fresh lemon or lime juice
½ cup all-purpose flour
3 large eggs, beaten
1½ cups panko breadcrumbs
Canola oil, for frying

1 recipe Cheesy Corn Grits (page 178)

Ingredients note: We often find folks comparing the flavor and texture of conch to abalone. Like abalone, or for that matter veal scallopine, conch must be pounded to render the meat tender. I use a meat pounder, placing the conch between sheets of plastic wrap. If you can't get conch you can subsitute sautéed shrimp.

Make the salsa rosa: Heat a large heavy saucepan over medium-low heat. Add the bacon and oil and cook until the bacon fat is fully rendered. Transfer the bacon to a plate to crisp up.

Add the butter to the oil and increase the heat to medium. Add the garlic and shallots and sauté, stirring occasionally, until lightly caramelized, 5 to 6 minutes. Stir in the sugar and cook for about 2 minutes. Add the red pepper flakes and vinegar and reduce by half. Add the chicken stock, turn up the heat to high and reduce by half. Add the tomatoes, season with salt pepper and bring to a boil.

Reduce the heat to low and cook, stirring, for about 10 minutes. Turn off the heat. Stir in the basil. Season with salt and pepper. If desired, puree in the blender, as I like to do.

Prepare the conch: Place the conch meat in a medium bowl, season with salt and pepper and marinate in the lemon juice for 30 minutes. Remove and pat dry. Place the flour, beaten eggs, and breadcrumbs in 3 separate shallow bowls. Dredge the conch in the flour, dip in the eggs, and dredge in the breadcrumbs. On a parchment-lined baking sheet, set aside the conch for a few minutes to allow time for the breadcrumbs to adhere.

Over medium heat, heat enough canola oil to coat the bottom of a large nonstick skillet. Fry the conch on each side until golden and cooked through. Transfer the conch to paper towels to drain, then cut into ribbons.

Spoon 3 tablespoons Salsa Rosa in the bottom of a large pasta bowl. Add grits as desired (and serve the rest on the side for your hungrier guests!). Top with the conch ribbons and serve.

MIDNIGHT SANDWICH

NVA: After a particularly long Friday night, nothing quite settles you down before bed or gets you going again in the morning like a well-spent half hour at Sandy's Café at the M&M Coin Laundry. A Midnight Sandwich at any time of day will get things back on the right track. The name of the wildly popular pressed sandwiches eaten around medianoche *(midnight) was coined by the late-night partygoers from Old Havana. JVA: Key West is gorgeous most mornings before the taxing midday heat sets in, so a breakfast eaten out-of-hand and possibly on a street corner, beach or bench is a great alternative to sitting down in an air-conditioned diner. For breakfast at Sandy's, they make these pressed sandwiches along the bacon/egg/cheese lines, but even if it's not the egg time of day, their namesake Sandy's Sandwich or classics like the Cuban Mix or* Medianoche *are sure to satisfy a ravenous appetite or simply "soak it up." They are open 24 hours, after all—and they deliver!*

Makes 1

1 small loaf Medianoche bread (a sweet, soft, egg-enriched bread; you can substitute Jewish Challah or Hawaiian bread)
Your favorite mustard
3 thin slices roast pork
3 thin slices sweet deli ham
3 thin slices Swiss cheese
Pickle slices
Unsalted butter, for pressing (optional)

Cut the bread horizontally in half. Spread a thin layer of mustard on one or both sides. On the bottom half of bread, layer the slices of roast pork, then the ham, and finally the cheese. Top with some pickle slices and then replace the top half of bread.

If a cold sandwich just ain't gonna do it, spread a little butter around the outside of the bread, wrap the sandwich up snugly in aluminum foil, and press it in a sandwich press.

No sandwich press? No problem. Place the sandwich in a frying pan over medium heat and use a heavy-bottomed pot or a brick double wrapped in foil to weigh it down. When the cheese is nice and melty and both sides are pressed and hot, your sandwich is ready to slice, traditionally on an extreme bias, and enjoy.

MUSHROOM-STUFFED "WHAMBURGERS"
WITH JANET'S FRIES

NVA: My wife makes the best burger I have ever eaten. In fact, almost anyone who has ever eaten one will attest to its supremacy. She grew up one of eight children. Her Dad, Irv, was the greatest Weber grill man in the county of Illinois where we grew up—his specialty was ribs and he liked big, robust flavors just like Janet. The burgers are cooked on our Weber grill where snow has never landed. She bastes them with our Lemon BBQ Sauce. Janet serves this whopping ten-ounce burger with her fries—and it's about all anyone can eat. Janet started making her "Whamburgers" so long ago, I'm not sure I can remember the first. But I look forward to the next and I pray it will be soon!

Serves 4

¼ cup Garlic Oil (page 172)
2 tablespoons unsalted butter
1 pound button mushrooms, thinly sliced
¼ cup sherry wine vinegar
2 pounds ground chuck beef, preferably 80% lean
Kosher salt and freshly ground black pepper
1½ cups Java Gal's Lemon BBQ Sauce (page 167)
4 of your favorite buns
Janet's Fries (page 174)

Heat the garlic oil and butter in a sauté pan over medium-high heat. When the butter starts to foam, add the mushrooms and cook until tender. Add the vinegar and stew the mushrooms for another 2 minutes. Using a fine-mesh strainer, pour the liquid into a small bowl; transfer the mushrooms to a plate and set aside.

Return the cooking liquid to the pan and reduce it over medium-high heat until it becomes syrupy. Add the syrup to the reserved mushrooms, mix, and let cool completely.

Meanwhile, divide the ground meat into four equal parts. Divide each part into two thick patties. Place ¼ cup of the sautéed mushrooms in the middle of four of the patties, leaving a border of meat all around. Put another patty on top of each, then crimp the outer edges of the patties tightly to seal and smooth the edges with your fingers. Refrigerate for about 1 hour to help seal the edges.

When ready to cook, season the patties with salt and pepper. Prepare an outdoor grill or preheat a grill pan over medium-high heat. Place the burgers on the grill and brush with some of the lemon BBQ sauce. After 5 to 7 minutes, flip the burgers, brush with more BBQ sauce and cook for another 5 to 7 minutes, depending on how well you like your burgers cooked. During the last 2 minutes of cooking, top the burgers with slices of your favorite cheese to melt. About 1 minutes before the burgers are done, add the buns, cut sides down, to the grill to toast.

Serve the burgers on the toasted buns with Janet's fries on the side.

> Ingredient Note: Janet insists on an 80/20 ratio of meat to fat. The meat is ground on the day she makes the burgers for her by our local butcher. The meat is never, ever frozen.

> Cooking Note: Janet sautés her sliced mushrooms, then she strains all of the liquid they've given off (push down and get it all!) and then reduces that liquid down to a mushroom "syrup," finally recombining it with the mushrooms. You will wonder why you never did this yourself once you try it.

THIRTY-SECOND SEARED BEEF SALAD
WITH SOY-LIME-CHILE DRESSING & SOBA NOODLES

NVA: Modern Key West is a much changed place from my early days on the island. But, then again, the polyglot mix of humanity that has long called Key West home defies easy categorization. One stroll through our graveyard and you will see that fact in stone: A man named Ling Hon, for instance, 1865 to 1946. The bright, bold and energizing flavors of a cool beef salad based on vivid Asiatic ingredients gives me the lift to handle the chore of trimming the never-ending palm leaves. Since this is a chilled salad it is great refreshment from any kind of work.

Serves 4

LEMONGRASS "TEA"
½ cup lemon juice
1 large stalk lemongrass, smashed
and roughly chopped

MARINADE AND STEAK
½ cup loosely packed fresh cilantro leaves
3 tablespoons seeded and chopped Serrano chiles
4 cloves garlic, minced
4 tablespoons light brown sugar
3 tablespoons fish sauce
½ teaspoon black pepper
Canola oil, as needed
One 12-ounce New York Strip Steak, cut into 4
equally thin steaks by your butcher on
an electric meat slicer
Kosher salt and freshly ground black pepper

SOY-LIME-GINGER DRESSING
3 tablespoons fresh lime juice
3 tablespoons soy sauce
2 tablespoons honey
1 tablespoons rice wine vinegar
1½ teaspoon mirin
2 teaspoons minced fresh ginger
1 tablespoon sesame oil
½ teaspoon chipotles chiles in adobo
½ cups pure olive oil
2 tablespoons chopped fresh cilantro leaves
2 tablespoons chopped fresh Italian parsley leaves
Kosher salt and freshly ground black pepper

Make the lemongrass "tea": In a small saucepan over a medium heat, combine the lemon juice and lemongrass. Cook until reduced by half. Pour through a strainer into a small bowl and discard the lemongrass. Set aside the infused lemon juice.

Make the marinade and steak: In a large bowl, combine all of the marinade ingredients. Add the reserved lemongrass "tea." Set aside until ready to dress the beef.

Heat a large sauté pan or wok over medium-high heat for a few minutes. Raise the heat to high and add enough of the oil to generously coat the bottom of the pan. Sear the steaks evenly on each side for no more than 30 seconds. Transfer immediately to a plate to cool completely. Season with salt and pepper.

Add the steaks to the prepared marinade. Chill in the refrigerator for 2 hours, turning once or twice. Cut the meat into bite-sized pieces, return to the marinade and set aside.

Make the dressing: In a blender, combine all the dressing ingredients except the oil and herbs and blend to mix. With the blender still running, slowly stream in the olive oil. Add the herbs and blend until smooth. Season with salt and pepper and set aside.

Make the soba noodles and vegetables: Cook the soba noodles in a large saucepan of boiling salted water until tender but still firm to bite, stirring occasionally. Drain in a colander, rinse under cold water and drain well. Transfer to a large bowl, add enough dressing to coat the beef and noodles without soaking them (any leftover dressing can be saved for another use). Cover and chill in the refrigerator.

SOBA NOODLES AND VEGETABLES
6 ounces soba noodles
Canola oil, as needed
12 shiitake mushroom caps, cleaned and julienned
Kosher salt and freshly ground black pepper
1 Serrano chile pepper, stemmed, seeded and minced
½ cup scallions, green and white parts, chopped
1 yellow bell pepper, stemmed, seeded and julienned
½ cup snow peas (or other green vegetable such as green peas or snap peas), blanched and julienned
½ radish, quartered and thinly sliced

Cook the sliced shiitakes over high heat in a nonstick skillet with just enough canola oil to keep them from sticking. Season with salt and pepper. Let cool completely. Transfer to a large bowl and toss with the Serrano, scallions, peppers, snow peas and radish. Add the beef along with the marinade, toss and chill in the refrigerator.

Divide the chilled noodles among four plates, creating a nest in the center of each serving. Place the beef and vegetables in each nest and serve.

"YARD BIRD" FRICASSEE

JVA: While sitting on a bench outside Key West Courthouse on Whitehead Street one morning, reading a book and generally minding my own business, I was suddenly approached by this menacing-looking red rooster. He had a fierce spur on the back of his leg, as the males of the species are well known to, and he was walking right at me, all puffed up. I noticed his brood pecking and scratching a few feet away and didn't see another rooster squaring up behind me—apparently he didn't like the cut of my jib and I had to go. He puffed up again and got close. We have a lot of wild chickens running around Key West, so I've seen these birds in a scrap or two and I didn't want any part of that. I backed off to fight another day. Here, now, is our revenge. This one's for you, Rodney . . .

Serves 6 to 8

8 chicken thighs, skin on, quickly rinsed and patted dry
Kosher salt and freshly ground black pepper
Bacon fat, or pure olive oil, for frying
3 tablespoons extra-virgin olive oil
1 sweet white onion, finely chopped
3 cloves garlic, finely sliced
1 Scotch bonnet or jalapeño pepper, stemmed, seeded and minced
1 tablespoon tomato paste
¾ cup dried currants
½ cup thinly sliced pitted green olives
½ cup thinly sliced pitted black olives
⅓ cup brine-packed capers, rinsed
Zest of 1 lemon
1 red bell pepper, finely chopped
1 tomato, chopped
1 cup Chicken Stock (page 161)
½ cup heavy cream

Preheat the oven to 350°F. Season the chicken thighs with salt and pepper and set aside.

Heat the frying fat of your choice in a heavy skillet over medium-high heat and sear the chicken on all sides. Place in the oven and bake until the chicken is cooked through and the juices run clear, 15 to 20 minutes. Transfer to a plate and set aside.

Put the same pan over medium heat. Add the olive oil, onion, garlic and pepper to the pan and cook until the onions begin to caramelize, 7 to 8 minutes.

Stir in the tomato paste and cook, stirring, until it turns a rust-like color. Stir in the currants, both types of olives, capers and lemon zest.

Stir in the red bell pepper, tomato and Chicken Stock. Make sure nothing is sticking to the bottom of the pan, then return the chicken to the pan and bring to a simmer. Cover, reduce the heat to medium-low, and cook until the tomato breaks down, 5 to 8 minutes.

OVEN-ROASTED MOJO CHICKEN

NVA: Most weekday dinners are about comfort meals; this Oven-Roasted Mojo Chicken is a favorite of mine. I've combined the mojo with sour orange, one of the most esteemed flavor providers of Cuba and several other of the Caribbean islands, in this extremely perfumed bird. It is best if marinated for two full days.

Serves 2 to 4

2 cups Sour Orange Mojo (page 168)
Kosher salt and freshly ground black pepper
One 3½-pound free-range chicken,
kosher or organic
Canola oil

Preheat the oven to 425°F.

Season the chicken all over with salt and pepper and place it in a large zip-tight bag. Pour 1½ cups of the mojo over the chicken and seal the bag, taking care to leave room for the mojo to move around within it. Marinate the chicken in the refrigerator for two full days if possible, but at least 8 hours, turning the bag occasionally to ensure that all of the chicken becomes saturated.

Transfer the chicken to a large bowl and allow the excess mojo to drip off. Discard the mojo. Tie the chicken's legs together with kitchen string.

Pour enough oil into a large sauté pan to coat the bottom and heat over medium-high heat. Sear the chicken evenly on all sides.

Place the bird, breast side down, on a roasting rack set in a roasting pan; cover loosely with aluminum foil.

Roast the chicken for 40 minutes then turn the bird over. Check for color; if it is not browning remove the foil for about 10 minutes, keeping an eye on the color and replacing the foil as necessary. The total cooking time is about 1 hour 10 minutes, or until the juices run clear and the interior temperature of the leg meat reaches 165°F on a meat thermometer. Let rest on a board for at least 10 minutes. Remove the strings and cut into quarters. Slice off the bones, if you like, to divide the white meat and the dark meat between your guests.

Warm the remaining ½ cup mojo. Serve the chicken with the mojo on the side.

Cooking Note: The key factor in cooking time is the weight of the bird. Even four ounces of difference in weight affects the time, so an instant-read or meat thermometer is a very worthwhile purchase. It will help you cook perfect roast chicken every time.

If you don't have a roasting rack you can cut up some onions and carrots and nestle the bird on top of them.

"BORN ON THE 4TH OF JULY" RIBS

NV A: While times have reduced the location of the Elks Club from a grand building on Duval to a former hardware and appliance store once named Mike's at 1107 Whitehead Street, the love of cooking by the Elks' members is going as strong as ever. For more years than I can remember, we have gotten many a Saturday afternoon fix for their BBQ ribs, always served with white bread, if we were not making our own rib-fest. Once we chat up the grill-and-smoke Grand Elk, Ken Sullivan, pictured at right, we like to head inside to the dark bar and enjoy a vibe akin to a classic Southern juke joint. Here is our take on the Elks Club's ribs. I made this spice rub for the first time on July the 4th. But we have been barbecuing ribs since childhood in our families.

Serves 4 to 6

SPICE RUB

¼ cup Kosher salt
¼ cup plus 2 tablespoons dark brown sugar
1 tablespoon ground cumin (best when freshly toasted and ground as most spices are)
1 tablespoon paprike
1 tablespoon allspice
1 tablespoon garlic powder
½ tablespoon ground cayenne
1 teaspoon ground chipotle chile pepper
1 teaspoon freshly ground black pepper
1 teaspoon smoked pimentón
1 teaspoon ground anise seed
1 teaspoon ground ginger

4 pounds back ribs
Java Gal's Lemon BBQ Sauce (page 174)

Combine all of the spice rub ingredients. Set aside about a quarter of the mixture and transfer the other three-quarters to an airtight container in a cool dark place for other rubbing occasions.

Lay the ribs out on a cutting board or other large surface and season the ribs with the rub on both sides, but more so on the meaty side. Set aside for up to four hours.

Prepare your grill: You need a medium-high heat to sear the ribs, then you'll need to bring it way down (to roughly 160°F to 175°F) and maintain a lower heat for 90 minutes or more. We've found that cooking the ribs a little longer and keeping the heat low and slow can help to focus the flavors and make for tastier, more caramelized ribs.

Once the grill is up to temperature, sear the meatier sides of the ribs until nicely burnished. Then flip the ribs and apply a layer of lemon BBQ sauce. Once the backsides are seared, turn down the heat, then flip and sauce again. Repeat the flip-and-sauce technique until the ribs are all but done.

Ingredient Note: It's high time to get into the fun that can be had when you make your own spice rubs and blends. It is almost always on a basis of slightly more sugar than salt and then you just riff from there, creating notes with any number of things in your spice rack.

MILK-BRAISED PORK TACOS
WITH QUICK-PICKLED RED ONIONS

NVA: The first time I saw this recipe was in the works of the great Marcella Hazan. I took Marcella's Italian idea into my Key West Kitchen and a new dish was born. Add Mexican crème fraîche, thinly sliced jalapenos, cilantro leaves and radish slices, if you like, to top each folded tortilla. JVA: This is a hero of a dish, perfect for get-togethers like Super Bowl Sunday because you do all of the prep beforehand. Besides reheating the pork with some of the braising liquid, covered, in a low oven, you'll want to make a fresh salsa and shred up some cabbage. Meanwhile, throw together some Quick-Pickled Red Onions (page 180)—they're ready to serve in an hour. When your friends and family are ready to eat, put out the salsa, sour cream, onions, pork, and some beautiful fresh tortillas.

Serves 10 to 12

One 5-pound fresh pork butt (shoulder), bone out
½ cup Escabeche Spice Rub (page 177)
¼ cup pure olive oil
1 sweet onion, roughly chopped
2 quarts whole milk
Kosher salt and freshly ground black pepper
1 Chayote, peeled if desired (or rinsed and dried), seeded and shredded
1 poblano chile pepper, stemmed, seeded and diced
Canola oil, for frying
20 to 30 corn tortillas
1 recipe Quick-Pickled Red Onions (page 180)

Place the pork butt in a large bowl and rub it on all sides with the spice rub. Let stand at room temperature for about 30 minutes. Meanwhile, preheat the oven to 285°F.

Heat a large heavy pan over medium heat. Add the olive oil and sear the pork on all sides, turning often, for 6 to 8 minutes, until browned. Add the onion and cook for 2 to 3 minutes, stirring. Add the milk.

Cut a crosshatch pattern in parchment paper or foil (to allow the heat to remain steady throughout cooking) and cover the pan loosely. Transfer to the oven and roast for 2½ to 3½ hours, without letting the milk get past a simmer, until the pork reaches an internal temperature of 145°F, and the meat is almost falling off the bone.

Remove the pork from the milk and set it aside on a board to rest. Pour the milk liquid into a clean heavy saucepan over medium heat and bring it to a simmer, skimming off the water and fat as it rises.

When all of the water and fat has been discarded, about 5 minutes, pour the milk liquid into a blender and puree—it will turn creamy—and set aside. This will yield about 4 cups, but you might not even need that much.

Slice, shred or chop the pork (the various sections and fat content of butts varies, so the method for deconstructing it will vary, too). Set aside in a bowl. Add enough of the creamy milk mixture to moisten the meat nicely; season with salt and pepper. Add the raw chayote and chile to the meat mixture. Stir and taste to adjust the seasoning.

Heat the canola oil in a large skillet over medium heat. Working in batches, fry the tortillas on both sides, fill them with the pickled red onions and the meat mixture, fold and fry again. Serve the tacos with the toppings of your choice.

Ingredient Note: Chayote
is a kind of squash. It
doesn't require peeling,
but a good scrub is
necessary. (Be sure it
is not waxed). After you
have split it in half and
removed the seeds, simply
shred it on a box grater.

"VEG HEAD" PILAU

NVA: We used to call the vegetarians who came into the restaurants "Veg Heads"—kind of like "Dead Heads." It wasn't derogatory, any more than the name for the legions of fans that worshiped the old San Francisco psychedelic/country band. They were, and are, a big community in Key West, and they didn't mind spending money on good food and, for that matter, good wine. Pilaus originated in India, evolved over to the Caribbean then on to Key West.

Serves 4

1 cup long-grain rice
2 tablespoons pure olive oil
2 tablespoons unsalted butter
2 cloves garlic, thinly sliced
½ large sweet onion, diced small
1 poblano chile, stemmed, seeded and minced
3 stalks celery, diced small
1 teaspoon paprika
¼ teaspoon cayenne pepper
1 ripe tomato, peeled and chopped medium
1½ cups Vegetable Stock (page 162)

GARNISH

3 tablespoons pure olive oil
1 red onion, thinly sliced
1 yellow bell pepper, thinly sliced
1 red bell pepper, thinly sliced

Rinse the rice under cold running water, strain it well, and set aside.

In a medium saucepan over low heat, melt the olive oil and butter. Add the garlic and stir. Increase the heat to medium and add the onion, chile and celery, season with salt and pepper and cook until the vegetables are soft, about 3 minutes. Add the paprika and cayenne and stir. Add the tomato and the drained rice and stir well. Add the vegetable stock and stir well again. Raise the heat to bring to a boil, stir, then immediately reduce the heat to low and cover the pot. Let the pilau cook until all of the liquid is absorbed, 10 to 15 minutes.

Meanwhile, prepare the garnish: Heat a large sauté pan over medium-high heat until very hot. Add the oil. When the oil is hot, add the onion and both kinds of peppers and sauté, stirring occasionally, until the vegetables are blistered, 8 to 10 minutes. Season with salt and pepper.

Spoon the rice into four dishes and top with the blistered vegetables. Serve hot.

EGGPLANT TOSTADAS

NVA: Tostadas *mean "toasts" in Spanish. I love toast. What I don't love is premade toast. The crispy warm outside and the pliant middle of just-made toast makes the experience much more sensuous. It's all about the timing—so prepare everything else and then make the toast. This tastes a lot like fantastic "pizza bread."*

Serves 4

2 tablespoons peanut oil
3 tablespoons unsalted butter
½ red onion, diced
1 small fennel bulb, diced
Kosher salt and freshly ground black pepper
½ tablespoon sugar
2 tablespoons Garlic Oil (page 171)
or pure olive oil
1 Japanese eggplant, peeled and cut
into 1-inch pieces
1 large tomato, peeled, seeded (if needed)
and roughly chopped
2 tablespoons tomato juice
¼ cup red wine
¼ cup red wine vinegar
2 tablespoons chopped fresh Italian parsley
¼ cup pitted and roughly chopped non-salty black
olives (niçoise or arbequina)
2 tablespoons small capers, rinsed
and roughly chopped
¼ cup pure olive oil
4 thick-cut slices Cuban bread or baguette,
using just the rounded side of the loaf
Freshly grated Parmesan, for garnish

In a large sauté pan over medium-high heat, heat 1 tablespoon peanut oil and 1 tablespoon butter. Add the onion and fennel and sauté until they just begin caramelize, about 8 minutes. Season with salt and pepper halfway through cooking. Add the sugar and cook until it glazes the vegetables, 1 to 2 minutes.

In a saucepan over medium-high heat, cook the eggplant in the Garlic Oil and the remaining 2 tablespoons butter. Season with pepper. When the eggplant is cooked through, 7 to 9 minutes, add it to the onion and fennel in the sauté pan and stir.

Wipe out the saucepan with paper towel and add the tomato, tomato juice, red wine, vinegar, and parsley, stir and bring to a medium-high simmer over medium-high heat. Reduce for 7 to 8 minutes to concentrate the flavor. Add the olives and capers, then immediately transfer to the eggplant mixture and stir gently.

Heat a large pan over medium-high heat, then add the oil. Lay the bread in the pan, cut sides down, and cook until golden on the cut sides. Transfer to paper towels to drain for a few minutes. Place the toasts on four plates, then divide the vegetable mixture among the toasts. Grate plenty of Parmesan on top and serve.

Ingredient Note: With the Japanese variety of eggplant, there is no need for the salting and weighting that causes more prep time and bother with regular eggplant.

MADURO FRITTATA WITH QUESO FRESCO

NVA: My comfort food mainstays often begin with eggs. My first job in a kitchen was as an egg flipper in a diner in Illinois. Instead of ruining eggs for me, it made me love them even more. And the first breakthrough ingredient that beckoned me down this Key West pathway of food was surely a caramelized plantain. Although they were exotic at the time, increasingly plantains are available in grocery stores. Plantains go through various stages of ripening when left at room temperature. (If you need to hurry them along, place them in a brown paper bag for a day or three). They can be served thinly sliced as "chips" when very green. They are used much like potatoes when mottled between green and black. When black, they are known as maduros *and are used for the caramelized babies we love so much. The skin of the plantains should be as black as licorice for this recipe. Serve this up with our Black Beans (page 163) on the side.*

Serves 4

2 very ripe plantains, peeled and cut diagonally into
¼- to ½-inch rounds
Kosher salt and freshly ground black pepper
Canola oil, for frying
4 ounces Queso Fresco, cubed
6 large eggs, lightly beaten with a pinch of salt
1½ tablespoons pure olive oil

Season the plantains with salt and pepper. Line a plate with paper towels.

Heat a large sauté pan over medium-high heat and pour in enough canola oil to coat the bottom of the pan. When hot, add the plantains and cook until deeply golden or browned. Transfer to the paper towels to drain.

Wipe out the pan with a paper towel and lower the heat to medium. Add the olive oil. When it is hot, add the cheese. Fry the cheese until golden brown on two sides, then pour in the beaten eggs.

When the eggs have begun to set on the bottom of the pan, arrange the plantain rounds on top, spacing them evenly. Lift the pan on an angle to allow the uncooked egg mixture to escape to the bottom of the pan to make sure all the liquid egg gets cooked.

When the eggs have fully set and can be easily detached from the pan, after 4 to 5 minutes, take a heavy round plate that is larger than the circumference of the sauté pan and invert it over the pan. Working over a table, quickly invert the pan onto the plate, then slide the frittata back into the pan and continue cooking on the second side for about 1 minute more.

Return the frittata to the plate and let settle for 5 minutes. Serve immediately or at room temperature.

FRIED GREEN TOMATOES
WITH PICKAPEPPA CREAM CHEESE

JVA: Now and then, folks stop by the house at cocktail hour. I can't help but throw together a couple of snacks for my friends. Fried Green Tomatoes with Pickapeppa Cream Cheese are quick and easy. Plus, the vinaigrette, the cornmeal dusting mixture, and the Pickapeppa Cream Cheese will all keep for nearly a month (and are quite versatile in their own right), so whip 'em up whenever you have a spare moment, just to have them on hand if company comes calling. Just slice, soak, dredge, fry and serve.

Serves 4

2 teaspoons Creole mustard
⅓ cup Champagne vinegar
⅔ cup canola oil
Kosher salt and freshly ground black pepper
1 to 2 green tomatoes cut into ¼-inch slices and lightly salted
½ cup whole-milk buttermilk
1 teaspoon Tabasco sauce
1 cup semolina flour
¼ teaspoon crushed red pepper flakes
¼ teaspoon cayenne pepper
3 cups canola oil, or more as needed, for frying

PICKAPEPPA CREAM CHEESE
4 ounces of cream cheese, softened
1 tablespoon Pickapeppa sauce
3 tablespoons sour cream
½ teaspoon lemon zest
½ teaspoon fresh lemon juice
⅛ teaspoon kosher salt
Pinch black pepper

Whisk the mustard and vinegar together in a large bowl. Gradually whisk in the oil. Add ¼ teaspoon salt and a pinch of pepper. Add the tomato slices to the vinaigrette and let marinate for at least 30 minutes, or up to 1 hour.

Meanwhile, in a medium bowl, combine all the Pickapeppa Cream Cheese ingredients and mix until well combined. Set aside.

In a small bowl, mix the buttermilk with the Tabasco sauce. In another bowl, mix the semolina flour with the red pepper flakes, cayenne, ¼ teaspoon salt and ¼ teaspoon pepper.

Heat the oil in a large pot until it reaches 350°F as measured by a deep-fry thermometer. One by one, remove the tomato slices from the marinade, shaking off any excess, and dip into the buttermilk mixture, then into the seasoned semolina flour to coat thoroughly.

Line a large plate with paper towels. Gently add the tomato slices to the hot oil and deep-fry for 3 to 5 minutes or until golden brown. Transfer to the plate to drain and season with salt and pepper.

Spoon the cream cheese mixture onto the bottom of four serving plates. Arrange the hot tomatoes on top and serve. Or place a smear of the cream cheese on the bottom of each plate and between each slice of tomato to create a stacked version.

GEORGIA PEACH & PECAN CRISP

JVA: When peaches are in season, one of my favorite desserts is something along the lines of this Georgia Peach and Pecan Crisp. But you don't have to wait, as this recipes uses canned peacehes. The streusel can be made ahead and frozen for up to 3 months or refrigerated for up to 1 week to keep on hand for whenever beautiful fruit comes your way. Apples, berries, or even sliced bananas are all wonderful substitutes—just cook them gently with just enough sugar, spices and juice to bring out their natural flavors, then cool them quickly to preserve their

Serves 4

PECAN SABLÉ
¾ cup sugar
¾ cups Georgia pecans, toasted and finely chopped
½ tablespoon unsalted butter
¼ teaspoon salt

STREUSEL
⅓ cup all-purpose flour
⅓ cup light brown sugar
½ teaspoon kosher salt
½ recipe Pecan Sablé (above), finely chopped
5 tablespoons unsalted butter, diced small and slightly chilled

Two 15-ounce cans Georgia peaches, drained (reserve juice for another use)
¼ cup packed light brown sugar

Make the pecan sablé: In a sauté pan over medium-high heat, cook the sugar until you reach 300°F on a candy thermometer. Stir in the pecans, then add the butter and salt. Pour into a glass or ceramic baking dish to cool completely.

Make the streusel: Place all of the streusel ingredients in a food processor and pulse until the butter is evenly distributed. It makes about 2 cups. Use immediately or refrigerate in an airtight container for up to 1 week.

Meanwhile, in a large skillet over medium heat, sauté the peaches with the brown sugar until the peaches are tender, but not falling apart. Transfer into 4 small ramekins (or one baking dish, if you prefer) and sprinkle the streusel evenly over each ramekin. Place underneath a hot broiler until the streusel bubbles and caramelizes nicely. Let cool for 5 minutes before serving.

RHUM CAKE

JVA: When that just-before-bed sweet tooth comes on, sometimes a tender slice of Rhum Cake does just the trick. Overstating the dominance of rum as the spirit of choice in this part—and other parts—of the world might just be absurd, but a slice of good Rhum Cake will assure even the staunchest of critics that all these "rummies" may have chosen their drink of choice well.

Serves 8 to 10

2½ cups (11 ounces) cake flour, plus more for the pan
1 tablespoon baking powder
½ teaspoon kosher salt
1 cup melted unsalted butter, plus more, chilled, for the pan
¾ cup granulated sugar
¾ cup light brown sugar
1½ cups sour cream
1 teaspoon vanilla paste
½ cup añejo rum
4 large eggs, at room temperature

GLAZE
¼ cup water, hot
3 cups confectioners sugar
½ teaspoon kosher salt
1 teaspoon pure vanilla extract
1 teaspoon key lime juice

Preheat the oven to 350°F. Grease a Bundt pan with chilled butter, then dust with flour to create a thin coat all the way around. (I like to wrap the pan with plastic so that I can turn it upside down and shake the pan to coat the tube in the center. Remove the plastic, and working over the trash can, tip the pan so that the flour falls out a little at a time as you continue to tap the sides while rotating all the way around to coat the sides up to the top.)

In a medium bowl, whisk together the cake flour, baking powder and salt. Make a well in the middle and set aside.

Place the butter, sugars, sour cream, vanilla and rum in a blender and blend until smooth. Stop the blender, add the eggs, stir briefly with a spatula, return the lid to the blender and just pulse once or twice to incorporate the eggs. Pour the blender mixture into the well of the dry ingredients. Fold the batter until just incorporated; some smooth lumps will remain.

Pour the cake batter into the prepared pan. Bake for 30 to 40 minutes, until the internal temperature of the cake reaches 195°F. Cool in the pan to room temperature, about 1½ hours.

Meanwhile, make the glaze: In a medium bowl, whisk the sugar into the water until fairly smooth. Add the salt, vanilla and lime. Whisk until completely smooth. Taste. If you like a little more lime or vanilla, whisk in a few drops.

Pour the glaze all over the top of your cooled cake. You can use as much or as little as you like.

SOUR CREAM-VANILLA ICE CREAM

JVA: Though this is a frozen custard–style ice cream, even denizen of the eggless Philadelphia style will appreciate the added tang and lift the sour cream give this frozen treat. A pastry chef friend of mine about my dad's age who grew up in Minnesota says it reminds him of the "sweet cream" ice cream he had as a kid. I haven't made it up to the Land of Ten Thousand Lakes yet myself, but somehow, I think I know what he means. Serve this up with the Georgia Peach and Pecan Crisp (page 145) or a slice of Rhum Cake (page 146).

Makes about 2 quarts

1 cup heavy cream
½ cup whole milk
¼ cup corn syrup
1 cup sugar
6 large egg yolks
1½ cups sour cream
2 teaspoons vanilla paste
2 teaspoons pure vanilla extract
¼ teaspoon kosher salt

Ingredient Note: If you can't find vanilla paste, you can scrape the insides of a nice fleshy vanilla bean and use that instead.

In a pot over medium-high heat, combine the heavy cream and milk and stir in the corn syrup and ½ cup granulated sugar. When the cream mixture reaches a scald, about 180°F as measured by a candy thermometer, turn off the heat.

In a large bowl, whisk the egg yolks and the remaining ½ cup sugar until pale and fluffy. Gradually introduce about half of the hot cream mixture to the yolks, stirring constantly. Pour the egg and cream mixture into the pot and heat over medium heat, stirring the bottom of the pot constantly with a heatproof rubber spatula to prevent sticking. When the mixture has reached 175°F, remove from the heat.

Fill a large container with ice water. Place the sour cream in a smaller glass or metal container, add the custard, vanilla paste and vanilla extract and stir in the salt. Place the container in the ice bath to chill, stirring frequently. Once cool, wrap with plastic and chill overnight.

Churn in an ice cream machine according to the manufacturer's instructions, transfer to a tightly sealed plastic container and return to the freezer until fully frozen.

JUSTIN'S BEST-EVER PEANUT BUTTER ICE CREAM

JVA: While apprenticing in the pastry department at Norman's, the pastry chef asked me if there was anything that I wanted to learn how to make. I thought for a moment, then asked, though a little embarrassed, "Can we make . . . peanut butter?" He happily obliged. Years later, when I finally got this ice cream recipe right, I felt like I had found the Holy Grail of Peanut Butter. Properly and perfectly roasting the peanuts, and quickly transferring them from the food processor, then to the cream to steep are the most critical steps of this recipe— that's where maximum peanutyness comes from. Everything else is straightforward. I use a coarse, then a fine strainer to remove the peanuts from the ice cream, as they will clog the fine one and the coarse one alone will let

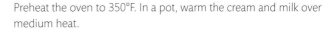

Makes about 1½ quarts

1 pint heavy cream
1 cup whole milk
One 12-ounce container skin-on Spanish peanuts
1 tablespoon corn syrup
1 cup sugar
1 tablespoon honey
6 large egg yolks
1 teaspoon kosher salt

Preheat the oven to 350°F. In a pot, warm the cream and milk over medium heat.

Spread out the peanuts on a sheet pan and roast in the oven until crunchy and toasted, 16 to 17 minutes, stirring the peanuts and rotating the pan halfway through. Let cool for 1 minute, transfer the nuts to a food processor and roughly chop; do not puree.

Immediately add the nuts to the pot containing the warmed cream. At this point, I like to let the peanuts steep for at least 30 minutes to allow the peanutty flavor to develop.

When you're ready, place the pot over medium-high heat and stir in the corn syrup and ½ cup sugar. When the cream reaches a scald, about 175°F, turn off the heat.

In a large bowl, whisk the yolks and the remaining ½ cup sugar until pale and fluffy. Gradually introduce about half of the hot cream mixture to the yolks, stirring constantly. Pour the egg and cream mixture into the pot and heat over medium heat, stirring the bottom of the pot constantly with a rubber spatula to prevent sticking. When the mixture has reached 175°F, remove from the heat and pour through a large-holed strainer and then a fine-mesh strainer into a glass or metal container to remove the peanuts from the ice cream.

Fill a large bowl with ice water. Stir the salt into the ice cream and set the container in the ice bath to chill. Once cool, wrap and chill overnight.

Churn in an ice cream machine according to the manufacturer's instructions, then place in a tightly sealed plastic container in the freezer until fully frozen.

TAMALE SCRAMBLE
WITH CHORIZO AND JACK CHEESE

JVA: A peek into my fridge at any given time will usually uncover some sort of homemade salsa. I tend to go with a variation on the roasted tomatillo-charred jalapeno-diced onion-cilantro route, but some decent bottled red tomato salsa or fresh pico de gallo will stand in proudly for this dish, as well—let's face it, it's early. Even a combination of some grape tomatoes, sliced in half, sprinkled with salt and pepper and a splash of vinegar, plus a little extra-virgin olive oil will make a big difference. Be sure to leave it for a bit to marry the flavors while you get the rest of breakfast together. Peanut butter and jelly. Peas and carrots. Tomatoes and eggs. Some things are just meant to be.

Serves 4 to 6

MARINATED TOMATOES
½ teaspoon roughly chopped fresh thyme
3 tablespoons extra-virgin olive oil
1 tablespoon balsamic vinegar
Kosher salt and freshly ground black pepper
18 ounces cherry tomatoes, cut in halves or quarters

2 corn husk– or banana leaf–wrapped corn tamales
5 large eggs
2 tablespoons whole milk
½ teaspoon kosher salt
½ teaspoon black pepper
4 ounces fresh chorizo
½ yellow onion, sliced
Jack cheese, shredded, to taste
Sour cream and hot sauce, for garnish

Make the marinated tomaotes: Mix together all of the ingredients except the tomatoes together in a bowl. Add the tomatoes, toss well and marinate for at least 30 minutes.

Place the tamales in a steamer basket over simmering water until thoroughly heated through.

In a small bowl, whisk together the eggs, milk, salt and pepper.

In a medium skillet over medium-high heat, crumble and brown the sausage. Transfer the cooked sausage to a bowl, reserving the rendered fat for another use. Without wiping the pan, add the onion and cook, stirring occasionally, until the onion are golden and translucent.

Add the onion to the egg mixture. Stir in the sausage and cheese and pour the mixture back into the skillet.

Now, moving swiftly, remove the hot tamales from the steamer and from their husk or leaf wrappers and place on individual plates.

Using a heat-proof rubber spatula, spin the eggs around in the pan, shaking the pan back and forth while rubbing the bottom of the pan to prevent sticking. (Turning the cooked curds around in the pan encourages quick but gentle cooking without browning or drying out the eggs.) When the eggs are just done (meaning the curds are set, not wet; done, but not by much), remove the pan from the heat and transfer the eggs to the dishes containing the unwrapped tamales.

Garnish the eggs with the marinated tomatoes, cheese, sour cream and your favorite hot sauce.

SOFT-SHELL CRAB PAN STEW
ON SAUSAGE-STUFFED FRENCH TOAST

NVA: If you think "sausage with crab" and worry, you might not have eaten enough New Orleans-style food. A long time ago, Emeril took us all to Ugelisch's little restaurant. (In New Orleans, it was Ugelisch's for funk and Commander's Palace for pomp—love that place, too.) Chef-owner Mr. Anthony laid bare the soul of Creole cookery at Ugelisch's. Though the restaurant is closed now, I still remember the flavors of dishes like Voodoo Shrimp, Muddy Water, Shrimp Gail and his barbecue shrimp. When I got back to Key West after one of those visits, I created this dish for a "Key West meets New Orleans" Sunday gospel brunch.

Serves 4

SAUCE
2 tablespoons unsalted butter
½ Scotch bonnet chile, stemmed, seeded and minced
¼ cup diced fennel
1 large shallot, roughly chopped
2 cloves garlic, finely chopped
1 bay leaf, broken
6 whole black peppercorns
1 tablespoon fresh thyme leaves
¼ cup Champagne vinegar
3 cups heavy cream
Kosher salt and freshly ground black pepper
1 tablespoon Dijon mustard

STEW
3 tablespoons unsalted butter
½ Scotch bonnet chile, stemmed, seeded and minced
1 clove garlic, minced
1 leek, white part only, diced
1 zucchini, diced
¼ cup diced fennel
1 cup farm-raised or wild mushroom caps, cleaned and evenly sliced
Kosher salt and freshly ground black pepper
¼ cup white wine
1 tomato, peeled, seeded and chopped

FRENCH TOAST
4 large eggs, beaten
1 cup half-and-half
½ teaspoon vanilla paste
¼ teaspoon mace
¼ teaspoon cinnamon
2 thick slices brioche
2 Italian sausages, cooked, cooled and thinly sliced
Clarified Butter (page 180)

First, make the sauce: In large heavy saucepan, heat the butter over medium heat until foamy. Add the chile, fennel, shallot and garlic and cook until soft. Add the bay leaf, peppercorns and thyme and stir. Add the vinegar and reduce by half. Add the cream and reduce over high heat until thick bubbles appear and the sauce is thick enough to coat the back of a spoon. Season with salt and pepper, whisk in the mustard and pour through a fine-mesh strainer into a small bowl. Keep warm.

Next, make the stew: In a large skillet, heat the butter over medium heat. Add the chile and garlic and let soften for 1 to 2 minutes. Stir in the leek, zucchini, fennel and mushrooms, season with salt and pepper and cook for 3 to 4 minutes, until fragrant. Add the wine and reduce until the liquid has almost evaporated. Add the tomatoes and heat through. Add the sauce and keep warm.

Then, make the French toast: In a large shallow dish, whisk together the eggs and the half-and-half. Add the vanilla bean, mace and cinnamon and mix well. Submerge the brioche slices in the egg mixture and let soak for 2 to 3 minutes.

Meanwhile, brush a griddle or large skillet with some clarified butter and heat over medium heat. Transfer the brioche slices to the griddle and cook on each side until golden on both sides. Transfer the slices to a work surface and wedge a few slices of the cooked sausage into each pocket. Place the brioche in a baking pan, cover the pan with aluminum foil and keep warm in a 300°F oven.

Lastly, dredge the crabs in the flour. Dust off any excess and set aside on a plate. Season lightly with salt and pepper. Heat a large skillet over medium-high heat. Add enough oil to coat the bottom of the pan. Crisp the crabs, starting with the flat side, until nicely golden. Flip over and cook for another 2 to 3 minutes until cooked through.

Spoon some of the sauce onto four warm plates, reheating if necessary, and top with the French toast. Place one soft-shell crab on top of each piece of French toast and serve.

SOFT-SHELL CRABS

4 medium soft-shell crabs, cleaned
Flour, for dredging
Kosher salt and freshly ground black pepper
Pure olive oil, for cooking

Cooking Note: You can
prepare the sauce and
stew a day in advance and
keep refrigerated until
ready to use. You can use
any extra sauce for pasta,
grilled fish or chicken.

Ingredient Note: Vanilla paste
is a great choice for dishes
like French toast. It's easy to
measure, consistent and flavorful.

GOLDEN PANCAKES WITH CITRUS CURD

JV A: Saturday nights can wreak havoc on Sunday mornings; if Dad ain't cookin', sometimes I'll head down for brunch at La Crêperie at the corner of Petronia and Thomas and let someone else handle my remedy. If I'm up early and making breakfast myself (it happens!) on a Sunday (I'm serious!), I'll whip up some Golden Pancakes with Citrus Curd to enjoy on the deck while watching the soft morning sunlight dance on the water's surface. A great thing about this recipe is that you can make up the pancake mix without the egg and buttermilk, keep it in the freezer, and use it to whip up pancakes in a matter of seconds any day of the week!

Serves 4 to 6

HOMEMADE PANCAKE MIX

1 cup plus 2 tablespoons old-fashioned rolled oats
1½ cups all-purpose flour
1 tablespoon sugar
1 tablespoon baking powder
2 teaspoons kosher salt
1 teaspoon cinnamon (I like to use a blend of cinnamon, nutmeg, and mace sometimes instead)
1 teaspoon baking soda
¼ cup canola oil

1 cup whole-milk buttermilk
1 large egg
Zest of 1 lemon
Zest of 1 orange
1 cup Homemade Pancake Mix (above)

CITRUS CURD

5 large eggs
1 cup plus 1 tablespoon sugar
1 cup mango puree
½ cup passion fruit puree
8 ounces (2 sticks) unsalted butter, chilled and diced
Fresh lemon or lime juice to taste
Pinch kosher salt

Diced fruit, for serving

Make the pancake mix: Place all of the ingredients except the oil in the bowl of an electric mixer and whisk by hand. Attach the beater to the mixer and drizzle in the oil while beating. The oil should be incorporated evenly, but will not make anything approaching a cohesive mass. Use immediately or freeze in an airtight container for up to 6 weeks.

In a blender, combine the buttermilk, eggs, lemon and orange zests and 1 cup of the pancake mix. Blend until nearly smooth. Pour into a plastic or glass container and chill in the refrigerator for at least 30 minutes.

Meanwhile, make the citrus curd: In a large bowl, whisk together the eggs, sugar, and both fruit purees. Place the bowl over a pot of simmering water, making sure the water does not touch the bottom of the bowl. Heat over the simmering water until the egg mixture thickens, whisking intermittently. Remove from the heat and whisk in the diced butter and salt. Taste and adjust the seasoning with a squeeze of lemon or lime juice or a pinch of salt. Store in an airtight container, with a piece of plastic wrap covering the surface to prevent a skin from forming, or use immediately.

Heat a griddle or large skillet over medium heat. Place a baking pan in the oven and preheat to 200°F. Once the griddle is hot, grease with cooking spray or clarified butter, if you have any on hand. Pour the batter for one pancake at a time in one motion and wait for a matte look around the edges and the appearance of a few bubbles, about 3 minutes, before flipping the pancake over to cook the other side for another minute. Transfer the finished pancakes to the warm pan in the oven and cover with a folded dry towel.

To serve, stack as many pancakes as you can eat on a plate, smearing each with some citrus curd. Sprinkle with diced fruit of your choosing.

LA BODEGA

Justin and I like to keep various "tools and jewels" stowed away in our kitchens that we can use to create more complex layers of flavors easily and frequently. Because these items are made in advance and kept on hand, we can choose to use them on a whim, regularly elevating our everyday meals to new heights.

Make a batch of several of the recipes in this chapter one afternoon when you have the time. Think of it as an investment with dividend of deliciousness and just tuck the little gems away until you're ready to put together a meal. When you have capable tools at your fingertips like the Red Onion Jam, Lemon BBQ, Old Sour Key Lime Magic, Escabeche Spice Rub, Smokey Oven-Roasted Tomatoes, and so on, you too can cook like we do, with little fuss, mess, or stress required.

We named this chapter La Bodega after one particular meaning of the word and this is, roughly, "the cargo hold of a ship." Many are familiar with the neighborhood convenience stores around some cities (like New York) referred to as "bodegas." There also happened to be a kind of gourmet retail store and deli in Key West during a long run of the 1980s called La Bodega. For us, the Bodega is an approach or mindset—the building up of our larder or pantry that gives us the authentic sources of flavors that are found from lands near and far.

Key West is a place out in the sea and the long history of sailors and trade merchants made it one exotic place for all kinds of comestibles. The thing I've tried to do in my work is to do more than create dishes; I have created a vision and version of an idealized Florida—one that exists as much in our shared experience, memory and imagination as it does in history. I began with the basic foods that not only filled my belly, but also made me grateful to have found myself in such a blessed place.

A NOTE ON STOCKS

Stocks offer us an opportunity as cooks to elevate the food we make and serve using, essentially, scraps and trim from meat and vegetables used in other preparations. Usually this means the butt (but not the roots themselves) and leafy ends of whole vegetables like heads of celery, carrots, onions (and their direct botanical relatives), often but not always simmered with the meaty, and ideally collagen-containing, bones of animals or fish.

Depending on the stock, there are several ways to arrange your cooking process. Roasting the bones and/or vegetables will deepen both color and flavor, but light stocks—in which the roasting is omitted—can distill a fine essence of the ingredients and keep your white sauce white. We almost exclusively roast for our stocks. We like our flavors BIG!

We provide three recipes for stocks here. Everyone does it a little differently it seems. Some simmer chicken stocks overnight, at a bare bubble, some simmer for just three hours. Some use a recipe, some just throw all the vegetable and/or meat scraps they happen to have on hand into a pot, cover with water and simmer it until it tastes like something. It may seem heresy, but honestly, they're all going to yield a product better than the water that brought them together—and better than paying someone to take it off your hands.

You win on both sides of the equation here. On one hand, you buy whole foodstuffs, which are cheaper

by weight. When celery is just hearts, and chicken is just thighs, we pay for someone to do the separation work and keep what's left. It's a lot like going to the jeweler to have a ring resized smaller. You pay them to take a little gold.

When we elect to break down the animals and vegetables ourselves, we pay less for them and always have leftover ends, leaves, wings, backs, fat, etc. which, given a few hours at a gentle simmer, can yield some "liquid gold," full of life-giving nutrients and the extracted essence of your loving attention.

BEEF STOCK

JVA: Beef stock is not something a lot of home cooks venture to make for themselves anymore. It's a commitment of time and effort that, for the most part, is alive and well only in professional restaurants. However, when a cow is harvested, it yields a lot more than just briskets, shanks and chuck steaks. There are many good parts to a beef cow, whose essence can be extracted into broth. Many dishes are just not as exemplory without its specific contribution. Braising tougher cuts like short ribs and oxtail in a combination of vegetables, red wine and beef stock underscores the deep richness of good beef.

Makes 3 quarts

4½ pounds beef neck bones
4½ pounds veal bones
¼ cup peanut oil
2 onions, roughly chopped
2 large carrots, roughly chopped
2 heads garlic, cut in half crosswise
4 large stalks celery, roughly diced
1½ to 2 gallons cold water
3 bay leaves, broken
20 fresh thyme sprigs
20 fresh Italian parsley sprigs
1 tablespoon black peppercorns

Preheat the oven to 425°F and set racks in the middle and lower.

Put the beef and veal bones in 2 large roasting pans and splash on the peanut oil. Don't crowd the bones or they won't get nice and dark. Roast for 30 to 45 minutes, rotating the pans about halfway through. Remove the pans from the oven, stir the bones and roast for 10 minutes more.

Add the onions, carrots, garlic and celery, stir and roast for about 50 minutes, until the vegetables get dark brown to slightly black.

Transfer the bones and vegetables to a large stainless-steel stockpot or divide them evenly between 2 large pots. (A relatively narrow one is best to avoid excessive reduction of liquids). Add 1 to 2 cups water to each roasting pan and, using a wooden spoon, scrape up the browned bits of meat and bone at the bottom. (Place the pans over medium-high heat to loosen the bits, if necessary). Add the browned bits to the bones and vegetables in the stockpot, then add enough of the remaining water to the pot to cover the bones.

Bring to a slow simmer and begin skimming the top to remove any fat and impurities. When the broth is cleared, add the bay leaves, thyme, parsley and peppercorns and simmer for 3 hours.

Let cool for a few minutes before thoroughly straining: First use a large-holed strainer, then use a fine-meshed strainer or cheesecloth. Chill the stock over ice thoroughly, without stirring. Using a skimmer, remove all the fat off the top of the stock. Refrigerate and use in 2 to 3 days. For longer storage, freeze for up to 6 months.

CHICKEN STOCK

NVA: When I'm asked during a cooking class what tips I can share, this one is at the top of my list: Make homemade chicken stock. Yes, they sell boxes of stuff marked "chicken stock" at the grocery store. But do you think the manufacturers really care about quality when you can't even see the bird? You can be sure most use poor-grade commercially raised creatures. We often call storebought stock "crayon water" in our kitchen; it has a color but it cannot illustrate. Your home-cooked food will achieve the structure of a professional kitchen's when you take the time to make your own stock. And if you are spending the money on organic, free-range or kosher birds, it is wise to use up every aspect of the animal. Soups and sauces are so much better when made with real chicken stock and once you start making it, you won't stop.

Makes about 7 cups

3 pounds chicken bones, preferably wings, backs, feet and/or necks
1 tablespoon pure olive oil
3 tablespoons unsalted butter
3 large carrots, roughly chopped
1 large onion, roughly chopped
3 large stalks celery, roughly chopped
1 head garlic, cut in half crosswise
8 ounces mushrooms, roughly chopped
1 cup white wine
10 to 12 cups water, or enough to cover the chicken bones
6 fresh thyme sprigs
6 fresh Italian parsley sprigs
6 fresh basil leaves
2 bay leaves, broken
1 tablespoon black peppercorns

> **Storage Note:** A good way to save space in your freezer and have the power of good beef or chicken stock at your fingertips is to reduce the defatted stock over medium heat to about a quarter of its volume, then chill the reduced stock in an ice bath, pour into ice cube trays and freeze. Once frozen, pop out the cubes of stock, put them in a labeled bag, and freeze.

Preheat the oven to 425°F.

Place the chicken bones in a roasting pan and roast, turning occasionally, until golden. Set aside.

Heat the oil and butter in a large stockpot over medium heat. When the mixture begins to foam, add the carrots, onion, celery, garlic, and mushrooms and stir to coat. Sauté the vegetables, stirring occasionally, until shiny and glazed, about 10 minutes.

Add the reserved chicken bones to the pot, top with a little ice, then add the white wine and water to cover, and bring just to a simmer—do not boil! As the mixture starts to foam, decrease the heat to low and skim off any fat and impurities. When the broth is fairly cleared, add the thyme, parsley, basil, bay leaves and peppercorns and simmer, uncovered, for 2½ to 3½ hours.

Remove from the heat and let the stock settle for about 10 minutes. Fill a large bowl with ice water.

Using tongs, pull the largest, heaviest pieces of bone out of the stockpot and discard. Place the stock into a stainless-steel bowl that's smaller than the ice bath. Place the bowl into the larger bowl of ice water to quickly chill the stock—do not stir. Once chilled, transfer to the refrigerator until a layer of fat has congealed on the top (a few hours or overnight).

Carefully remove this fat, then transfer the stock to airtight containers and refrigerate for up to 5 days, or freeze for up to 6 months.

VEGETABLE STOCK

There is a simple decision to make when you begin to make this stock: Do you want it to be darker in color (from the process of caramelization, which makes it a little more sweet) or do you wish to use it for dishes you want to keep lighter in color (like a vegetarian cream soup or sauce)? If you want it dark, allow the root vegetables to cook for 10 to 15 minutes in the oil and butter to bring out the color, and then continue with the rest of the recipe.

Makes 3 quarts

4 tablespoons pure olive oil
2 tablespoons unsalted butter
2 heads garlic, cut in half crosswise
2 onions, diced
2 leeks, white and green parts, diced
3 to 4 large carrots, peeled and diced
6 stalks celery, diced
1 bulb fennel, diced
1 ounce dried mushrooms, preferably porcini, or a mix of varieties, soaked in warm water (optional)
8 ounces button mushrooms, roughly chopped
2 tomatoes, cored and roughly chopped
6 fresh thyme sprigs
12 fresh basil leaves
12 fresh Italian parsley sprigs
1 bay leaf, broken
1 tablespoon black peppercorns, toasted and bruised
1 teaspoon salt
14 cups water

Heat the oil and butter in a large heavy stockpot over medium heat. Add the garlic, onions, leeks, carrots, celery and fennel and cook to your desired color (see above).

Drain the dried mushrooms and add them, along with the fresh mushrooms to the pan. Add the tomatoes, thyme, basil, parsley, bay leaf, peppercorns, salt and water. Bring to a boil over medium-high heat, skim and simmer for 1 hour.

Strain through a fine-mesh strainer into a bowl set inside an ice bath to cool. Transfer the stock to airtight containers and refrigerate for up to 7 days or freeze for up to 2 months.

> **Cooking Note:** If you net more than 3 quarts, return the stock to the stovetop and reduce it to 3 quarts over medium heat.

BLACK BEANS

Cucina povera is an Italian phrase that means "cooking of the poor." The most resourceful cooks are mothers and grandmothers who have learned how to evoke the full power of food despite a largesse of expensive ingredients. As I've become more aware of the finite resources of our planet, I've made some changes to my cooking. I used to make black beans using more elaborate recipes and an abundance of stock, but this one is now my go-to version. The flavors are pure and simple, yet deep and satisfying. Omitting the ham hock and bacon fat is fine if you're looking for a vegetarian option here.

Serves 4

4 cups black beans (one 16-ounce package)
4 cups water, plus more as needed
1 smoked ham hock
2 tablespoons bacon (or duck) fat
¼ cup pure olive oil
1 tablespoon unsalted butter
4 cloves garlic, thinly sliced
1 to 2 jalapeño peppers, depending on desired heat, stemmed, seeded and minced
1 cup minced sweet onion
1 tablespoon toasted and freshly ground cumin
2 tablespoons sherry wine vinegar
1 bay leaf, broken
Kosher salt and freshly ground black pepper

> **Cooking Note:** If using a pressure cooker is not an option, simply simmer the beans, uncovered, stirring occasionally and topping off with water as needed to keep them covered, until tender, 2 to 3 hours.

Wash the beans thoroughly and put them in a saucepan or a bowl. Cover with the water and allow them to soak for about 4 hours. The beans will swell up as they soak; discard any that float to the top.

Strain the beans, discarding the water they soaked in and rinse them off. Transfer the beans to a pressure cooker and add enough water to cover them by 2 inches. (Always make sure to follow the manufacturer's instructions on filling your pressure cooker appropriately!) Add the ham hock. If you have pressure settings, make sure it is set to the right one for black beans. Attach the lid of the pressure cooker and place over a medium-high heat until it begins to hiss, then lower the heat for a steadily chirping stream of steam. Simmer for 30 to 40 minutes, but this can vary. Set aside off the heat. When the pressure drops and it is safe to open the top, check the beans. (Add more hot water from time to time if needed but no salt during this initial process as it can make the beans toughen.)

Meanwhile, heat a heavy-bottomed pan or skillet over medium heat. Add the fat, oil and butter. When the butter has melted, add the garlic and jalapeños and cook, stirring, for 3 to 4 minutes to build flavor.

Add the onion and cumin, stir to coat and cook until caramelized, stirring only occasionally, about 10 minutes. When the vegetables are nicely caramelized, add the ham hock, vinegar, beans (and the liquid they cooked in) and bay leaf and season with salt and pepper. Reduce the heat to medium-low and cook, uncovered, for about 20 minutes.

Discard the ham hock, or if the ham hocks are really meaty, take the time to pull the meat off and add it to the beans. Using scissors, remove and discard any tough rind. If you want creamier black beans, you can puree a portion of the beans and return it to the pot. Simmer gently, stirring occasionally, adjusting seasoning as necessary, until the beans are tender and the mixture has thickened to your liking.

CHIMICHURRI ROJO

JVA: Chimichurri rojo, and it's somewhat more common cousin chimichurri verde (a green version made with parsley), are usually served as piquant or herbaceous accompaniments to earthy grilled meats, such as skirt steaks, duck breats, chicken and even hamburgers. They also add an incredible zing to a basic mayonnaise or can be beaten into whole butter, chilled, and then used instead of regular butter for everyday things like frying eggs (go ahead and try it—you'll make it a habit, I promise).

Makes ¾ cup

¼ cup pure olive oil
½ cup sherry wine vinegar
1½ tablespoons hot paprika
2 teaspoons cayenne pepper
4 cloves garlic, minced
1 teaspoon freshly ground black pepper
1 teaspoon cumin, freshly toasted and ground
1 bay leaf, broken in half
½ teaspoon kosher salt

Combine all of the ingredients in a bowl and whisk together until well combined. Transfer to an airtight container and refrigerate for up to 4 weeks.

COCKTAIL SAUCE

NVA: If I had to name two weather vanes that measure our cooking, I'd say "acidity" and "heat." It is also a given that we have meaty notes, since we cook so many dishes centered around protein in our kitchen—even many of our vegetable dishes have a meaty power. So, while we don't typically strive for really spicy (although in some occasions we do), we very often are looking for something refreshing and lifting, even in a simple, everyday kind of sauce. Spice and acidity are the buttons to push, and in this cocktail sauce, you will notice the greater clarity they offer. Every bite counts. Every scintilla of what goes into cooking matters.

Makes 1⅔ cups

1½ cups ketchup
5 tablespoons prepared horseradish
1 teaspoon fresh lemon juice
1½ teaspoons Pickapeppa sauce

Mix together all of the ingredients in a bowl. Transfer to an airtight container and refrigerate for up to 4 weeks.

RED ONION JAM

We suggest you use this savory jam in our Mollete Sandwich (page 63) but it is a brilliant partner to many savory dishes. Try it with hamburgers, grilled sausages, roast or even fried chicken.

Makes 2 cups

¼ cup pure olive oil
3 medium red onions, minced
Kosher salt and freshly ground black pepper
⅔ cup sherry wine vinegar
2 tablespoons unsalted butter
½ cup sugar

Heat a large saucepan over medium heat. When hot, add the oil then the onions and season with salt and pepper. Toss well then allow the onions to caramelize, tossing now and then, to ensure even cooking.

When the onions turn translucent then begin to caramelize, deglaze with the vinegar, cooking down until all the liquid is almost gone, then add the butter and sugar and stir well. Cook, stirring occasionally, until the mixture thickens to where very little liquid remains and it begins to hiss when stirred.

When you've reached your desired consistency, remove the pan from the heat and transfer the jam to a clean glass jar. Alternatively, let the jam cool before transferring it to a bowl to cool completely. Refrigerate in an airtight container for up to 3 months.

MANGO CHUTNEY

NVA: The Redlands, as they are called, and the area south of Miami up to where the mainland ends is an area of great agricultural activity. We love to jump in the jeep and drive out of the city to visit—every time we go I wonder why we don't go more often. The land is very flat and produces a range of fruits and vegetables, including an astounding variety of mangos, which are the primary ingredient in this recipe. This chutney is spicy-ish! If you want to start less spicy, simply add fewer Scotch bonnets.

Makes 1 quart

7 cups peeled and diced mango
2 cups apple cider vinegar
1 cup granulated sugar
1 tightly packed cup dark brown sugar
1 cup red onion, diced
3 to 4 Scotch bonnet chiles, stemmed,
seeded and minced
1 tablespoon minced fresh ginger
½ tablespoon cinnamon
1 teaspoon ground allspice

Combine all of the ingredients in a mixing bowl and refrigerate overnight to let the flavors develop.

The next day, transfer the mango mixture to a large heavy saucepan and slowly bring it to a slow boil over medium heat. Reduce the heat to low and simmer for about 1 hour.

Remove from the heat and let the chutney cool before transferring it to a bowl to cool completely. Transfer to an airtight container and refrigerate for up to 1 month.

Storage Note: If you want to keep the chutney for a longer period of time, you will need to can it according to the jar manufacturers' safety instructions.

CHAMPAGNE VINAIGRETTE

NVA: Here is a classic, light and supportive dressing that you can use in a fairly limitless manner. We use it twice in Chapter 3, for the Port of Call Crab & Avocado Salad (page 92) and the Grilled Duck Breasts (page 94). Feel free to substitute other wine or fruit-based vinegars in it, if you prefer.

Makes 3 cups

1 teaspoon kosher salt
½ teaspoon black pepper
2 tablespoons Creole mustard
1 cup Champagne vinegar
2 cups canola oil

In a medium bowl, whisk together the salt, pepper, mustard and vinegar. Gradually add the oil while continuing to whisk, until well mixed.

Taste and adjust the seasoning with salt and pepper, if necessary. Transfer to an airtight container and refrigerate for up to 3 weeks.

JAVA GAL'S LEMON BBQ SAUCE

NVA: This yields a generous amount of BBQ sauce, but it is easier to make it in one big batch than to make it often—and it lasts months in the fridge as most BBQ sauces do. This one will disappear more quickly than some, though, because you will not be able to resist putting it on just about everything! Please note that this recipe does not need any salt and pepper. P.S. Java Gal is Janet Amsler Van Aken and she deserves the credit for this recipe.

Makes 2 quarts

4½ lemons, cut in half
3 sweet onions, cut in half
½ cup dark brown sugar
½ cup chiles mezcla
¼ cup toasted whole cumin seeds
½ cup dried chipotle chiles,
stems and seeds included
12 quarts plus ½ cup of water
½ cup ketchup
¾ cup Worcestershire sauce
1½ tablespoons Tabasco

In a mixing bowl, combine the lemons, rinds and all, onions, brown sugar, chiles mezcla, cumin, chipotle chiles and water and mix well. Transfer to a large, heavy pot over medium heat and reduce until the lemons are completely soft.

Pour the lemon mixture through a fine-mesh strainer into a clean saucepan and reduce again until you're left with 1 quart liquid.

Add the ketchup, Worcestershire and Tabasco and mix well. Pour into a clean glass bottle or Mason jar and store in the fridge for up to 6 months.

GINGER-SOY DRESSING

JVA: I've used this recipe for years, as a salad dressing and as a marinade for meats and vegetables. But recently I discovered that my appreciation for this combination of soy (salt), vinegar/reduced orange juice (acid tempered with sweet), shallots/garlic/ginger (Asian aromatics), cilantro (herbaceous), and sesame oil (ethereal/undeniable) was deep in my bones. Recently when I wanted a sauce to coat fried chicken wings, a reduction based on this Ginger-Soy Dressing (with honey and sugar for stickiness and Sriracha for extra spice) provided the only

Makes 1 quart

4 cups fresh orange juice, reduced to 2 cups
3 large cloves garlic, minced
3 tablespoon minced fresh ginger
3 tablespoons minced fresh cilantro leaves
1 teaspoon kosher salt
1 teaspoon toasted and freshly ground black pepper
1 cup red wine vinegar
1 cup light soy sauce
1 cup sesame oil
1 tablespoon chili oil

In a saucepan over medium-high heat, cook the orange juice for 15 minutes, until reduced to 2 cups. Set aside to cool.

Transfer the reduced juice to a mixing bowl, add all of the remaining ingredients and whisk to thoroughly combine. Transfer to an airtight container and refrigerate for up to 3 weeks.

SOUR ORANGE MOJO

NVA: In many places, fresh sour oranges are not available. That can be overcome. Simply juice equal parts lime and orange to create a good replacement. If you do have access to sour oranges, you probably have heard of this classic Latin-Caribbean sauce called "mojo." It is one of our favorite things to make, cook with and teach.

Makes about 3 cups

12 cloves garlic, minced
2 Scotch bonnet chiles, stemmed, seeded and minced
1 teaspoon kosher salt, plus more for seasoning
4 teaspoons whole toasted cumin seeds
2 cups extra-virgin olive oil
⅔ cup fresh sour orange juice
4 teaspoons sherry wine vinegar
Freshly ground black pepper

In a mortar with a pestle, mash the garlic, chiles, salt and cumin together until fairly smooth. Scrape into a bowl, add a third of the olive oil and set aside.

Heat the remaining two thirds of the oil in a small saucepan over medium heat until fairly hot, then pour it over the garlic-chile mixture. Let stand for 10 minutes.

Whisk in the sour orange juice and vinegar. Season with salt and pepper. Place in a glass jar or airtight container and refrigerate for up to 3 months.

OLD SOUR KEY LIME MAGIC

NVA: The old Conch folks use this on so many items, it is hard to think of something not to use it on. Shaking it on ny type of fish dish, of course, is the most common use. If you don't have key limes handy, substitute Persian limes.

Makes about 2 cups

2 cups fresh key lime juice
1 tablespoon kosher salt
A few drops hot sauce

In a small bowl, mix all of the ingredients then set aside at room temperature for a day or so to let the flavors develop.

Strain through a cheesecloth 3 or 4 times to remove all of the salt. Transfer to a clean Mason jar or bottle with a stopper and refrigerate for 2 weeks to cure before using. It keeps in the refrigerator for up to 2 months.

ICE BOX CUCUMBER PICKLES

JVA: Having too much of a good thing can cause anxiety if those good things are perishable. However, if those perishable things are pickle-able, then the occasional glut of your favorite fresh vegetable can be a very rewarding thing, indeed. Pickling and preserving have become very popular once again, and thank goodness, because having a variety of pickled items, featuring a variety of flavor options, on hand can put you well ahead of the game when it comes time to make a meal.

Makes about 2 cups

1 European (hothouse) cucumber, peeled and thinly sliced
1 tablespoon kosher salt
3 tablespoons sugar, or more or less to taste
½ cup Champagne vinegar
½ teaspoon cayenne pepper

Toss the cucumber with the salt in a strainer over a bowl. Let drain for about 30 minutes to remove excess liquid, then rinse well. Spin in a salad spinner or lay out on paper towels to drain.

In a mixing bowl, combine the sugar, vinegar and cayenne and stir well. Add the cucumber slices and toss to coat them on all sides, and marinate for 15 to 20 minutes before serving.

QUICK-PICKLED SHIITAKE MUSHROOMS

NVA: This simple pickle is great with grilled fish, steaks, burgers or in vegetarian dishes, including chilled noodle salads. Don't forget to save the mushroom stems for vegetable stock, see page 162.

Makes about 1⅓ cups

Peanut or canola oil
24 shiitake mushrooms, caps only, cleaned of any dirt and thinly sliced
4 tablespoons sugar
2 tablespoon soy sauce
1 jalapeño pepper, stemmed, seeded and minced
2 tablespoons minced fresh ginger
2 tablespoons sherry wine vinegar

Pour enough oil in a nonstick skillet to coat the bottom and heat over medium heat. Add the shiitakes and cook until just tender. Let cool.

In a mixing bowl, combine the sugar, soy sauce, jalapeño, ginger and vinegar and whisk to combine. Stir in the cooled mushrooms. Taste for seasoning, but they should be nicely seasoned as is! Place in an airtight container and refrigerate for up to 2 weeks.

GARLIC OIL AND ROASTED GARLIC

JV A: Keeping these two essentials—both products of the same simple preparation—on hand in our kitchen is like making sure we have salt, butter, milk and bread. They are so essential and basic to everything we cook, that when we move to a new place, it's generally the first thing we make—except for maybe a pot of coffee.

Makes about 4 quarts Garlic Oil and
¾ cup Roasted Garlic

8 heads garlic, cut in half crosswise
12 fresh thyme sprigs (or a blend of dried herbs)
12 black peppercorns
3 bay leaves, broken
4 quarts pure olive oil

Preheat the oven to 275°F.

Arrange the garlic, cut side down, in a 4-quart ovenproof saucepan. Add the thyme, peppercorns and bay leaves. Pour the oil over the garlic and cover. Roast in the oven for about 1 hour and 15 minutes, but check after 40 minutes—a few bubbles are okay, but if the oil is simmering the garlic will become dark, sticky and bitter. The garlic is done when you can easily pierce the cloves with the tip of a small sharp knife. If necessary, cover and return to the oven, checking for doneness every 5 minutes.

Transfer the garlic mixture to a colander set over a bowl then strain the oil through a cheesecloth or fine-mesh sieve into a heatproof jar and keep in a cool dark place for up to 1 month. Allow the garlic to finish draining in the colander.

While the garlic is still warm, but cool enough to handle, use a small knife to pop the garlic cloves out of their paper husks. Refrigerate in an airtight container (mash if desired) for up to 6 weeks.

GARLIC OIL ROASTED POTATOES

JV A: When my mom makes these potatoes, she roasts them until just done at a medium temperature, then finishes them at a higher temperature to crisp the outsides to perfection. You would swear she cooks them in butter, but no; just Yukon gold potatoes, garlic oil, salt, and pepper. They're finished just inside of an hour with very little fuss. But wait, it gets better. You can also roast the wedges until just done, let cool and then refrigerate in an airtight container, saving the higher temperature roasting for when you're ready to serve the potatoes.

Makes as much as you desire

Yukon gold potatoes, scrubbed and cut into wedges
(6 to 8 wedges per potato, depending on size)
Garlic Oil (see above) or pure olive oil
Kosher salt and freshly ground black pepper

Preheat the oven to 350°F. Place the potato wedges in a large bowl. Pour in enough oil to coat the potatoes, then season with salt and pepper and toss well.

Transfer to a baking dish and roast until cooked through, 25 to 35 minutes. Remove from the oven, increase the heat to 425°F and return to the oven. Taking care that the potatoes don't burn, let them get good and crispy on the edges before scraping and flipping them over. When they are crispy all over, about 15 minutes, serve immediately.

JANET'S FRIES

NVA: I first had Janet's handmade fries in her parents' home while she was still in high school, and I've been loving them since. Never have I had a better fry.

Serves 4

1½ pounds Idaho potatoes
Peanut or canola oil, for frying
Kosher salt and freshly ground black pepper

Scrub the potatoes in cold water and pat them dry. Cut each potato into finger-size strips, leaving the skins on. Soak them in a large bowl of cold water for at least half an hour or as long as overnight to pull out the starch. Remove the fries from the water with your hands and spread them out to dry on a towel before frying.

Fill a heavy pot about halfway up the sides with the oil—this is a safer method than a full pot. Heat the oil over medium heat until you reach about 200°F on a deep-frying thermometer. Lower the fries into the oil—we don't use a fryer basket but you surely can. If you're using a basket lower it into the oil without the fries first to prevent sticking. Then, add the fries to the basket and lower it in. Keeping the oil temperature steady, fry the potatoes for about 15 minutes. Transfer the fries—they will be somewhat limp when you lift them—to a tray lined with plenty of paper towels to drain. At this point they can keep in the fridge for up to a week.

When you are ready to serve, increase the heat to high and bring the oil to 360°F. Lower the fries into the oil and stir gently. Replace the paper towels. Cook the fries for about 1 minute, until golden brown and crispy.

Transfer the fries to the paper towels and season with salt and pepper, if desired. Shake them around to distribute the seasoning and serve immediately.

Cooking Note: We do the twice-fried method here for extra crispiness.

YELLOW RICE

NVA: It is much more common to see rice in dishes in Key West than the potatoes I ate along with many meals growing up in the Midwest. And the rice is yellow about half of the time. Because of its strong Spanish roots, yellow rice was prized in part due to its association with saffron, which is more precious than gold. That said, often the home cooks in Key West used a spice mix called bijol instead. Invented in the 1920s in Cuba, bijol is made from a mix of corn flour, annatto powder, cumin and "color." This collection of ingredients was more affordable while still supplying the drama of saffron. I have eaten my share, but now I more often than not include that small pinch of good saffron and I'm happy. In any Cuban restaurant, you are offered beans and rice and the colors and types of rice will vary. But almost every entrée comes with rice of some kind, so you cannot go wrong serving this recipe with just about any dinner featuring Latin flavors.

Makes 3½ to 4 cups

1½ cups warm Chicken Stock (page 161)
½ teaspoon Spanish saffron
2 tablespoons pure olive oil
2 tablespoons unsalted butter
1 jalapeño pepper, stemmed, seeded and minced
4 cloves garlic, minced
½ onion, diced
1 carrot, peeled and diced
1 stalk celery, diced
2 small bay leaves, broken
1 cup long-grain white rice
Kosher salt and freshly ground black pepper

Place the stock in a small bowl and add the saffron to soften. Set aside.

In a saucepot, heat the oil and the butter over medium heat. Add the jalapeño and garlic, stir and cook for 15 seconds. Add the onion, carrot, celery and bay leaves and stir well. Cook until the vegetables are well glazed, about 10 minutes, stirring frequently.

Add the rice, season with salt and pepper and stir well. Add the chicken stock and saffron and stir once. Bring almost to a boil and then immediately lower the heat to low. Cover the pot and cook until all of the stock is absorbed, 10 to 15 minutes (steam holes will be a sure sign that the rice is cooked, but tip the pot a bit to see if any stock is visible).

CALYPSO SPICE RUB

NVA: The original meaning of calypso is "she that conceals." Then it became the name of a dance or song that emigrated from Africa. Funny how things change! I like to think this Calypso Spice Rub adds a dance beat to our cooking. We use it when we want a bit more heat than the Escabeche Spice Rub, below, provides.

Makes about ⅔ cup

2 tablespoons cumin seeds
1 tablespoon coriander seeds
1 tablespoon yellow mustard seeds
1 tablespoon cloves
2 tablespoons black peppercorns
1 tablespoon powdered ginger
1 tablespoon ground cinnamon
2 tablespoons dark brown sugar
2 teaspoons kosher salt
1 tablespoon ground ancho chiles, stemmed and seeded

In a dry skillet over medium heat, toast the cumin, coriander and mustard seeds, the cloves and black peppercorns. Transfer to a mortar and pestle or spice grinder and grind fine.

Place the spice mixture in a small bowl, add the slat and ground ancho chiles and mix well. Transfer to an airtight container and store in a cool dark place for up to 1 year.

ESCABECHE SPICE RUB

NVA: I began making this spice rub in the 1980s. It may have been when I was creating the original template for New World Cuisine at Louie's Backyard. This straightforward combo of spices provides a mighty tempting open door to walk into Flavorland. Recently, a young Cuban cook who works in my kitchen floored me when he told me he cooked pork at home using this spice—and now his Cuban-born grandmother has embraced it in her cooking!

Makes about 1¾ cups

1 cup black peppercorns
1 cup cumin seeds
½ cup sugar
¼ cup kosher salt

Toast the peppercorns in a dry skillet over medium heat, shaking the pan frequently until the peppercorns are fragrant and slightly smoking, about 1 minute. Remove to a bowl or tray to cool briefly. Repeat the process with the cumin seeds over medium-low heat, tossing a little more frequently and for a little less time.

Transfer the toasted spices to a spice grinder and grind fine. Transfer to a bowl and mix in the sugar and salt. Store in an airtight container in a cool dark place for up to 1 year.

CHEESY CORN GRITS

NVA: Growing up in the north, I didn't learn to appreciate grits until Justin ordered them, so matter of factly for breakfast one morning at Blue Heaven in Bahama Village. He has a talent for getting me to try things his way— now I'm a fan, too!

Serves 4

3 cups whole milk
1 cup water
1 tablespoon kosher salt, plus more for seasoning
1 teaspoon finely ground black pepper, plus more for seasoning
8 tablespoons (1 stick) unsalted butter, cut into small pieces
1 cup fine grits or polenta flour
½ cup grilled or sautéed corn kernels
2 to 3 jalapeño peppers, stemmed, seeded and minced
1 cup shredded queso blanco

In a heavy saucepan over medium-high heat, combine the milk with the water, salt, pepper and butter and bring just to a boil. Whisk in the grits and stir constantly. After about 3 minutes, when the grits start to bubble and "splat," lower the heat to medium-low and mix in the corn and jalapeños. Stir often to prevent sticking.

When the grits are thick and cooked through, about 25 minutes, add the cheese and whisk vigorously for 1 minute. Turn off the heat and continue to whisk for 1 more minute. Season to taste and keep warm until needed.

BLISTERED CORN

JVA: Blistered corn has been a regular side dish on our table for as long as I can remember. It happily complements any number of dishes such as Oven-Roasted Mojo Chicken (page 133), Chuletas Empanizadas (page 68), Mango BBQ'd Swordfish (page 118), and, of course, Mushroom-Stuffed "Whamburgers" (page 127). It can even garnish soups like the Caramelized Plantain Soup (page 31), or get stuffed into the Mollete Sandwich (page 63) for a little sweet crunch. Not long ago, I reduced a little cream, added this blistered corn and a touch of sugar and more salt, and after simmering it together for a couple of minutes, pulsed it in the food processor: Best. Creamed. Corn. Ever.

Serves 4

2 tablespoons canola oil
2 tablespoons unsalted butter
4 cups corn kernels (from 6 to 7 ears of corn)
Kosher salt and freshly ground black pepper

Heat a sauté pan over medium-high heat. Add the oil and butter, then swirl to melt. Add the corn, season with salt and pepper, and toss. Sauté the corn, stirring after 2 to 3 minutes so that some initial caramelization can take place. Stir once or twice more until nicely colored, about 5 minutes total. Season again with salt and pepper if desired.

QUICK-PICKLED RED ONIONS

JV A: Like the Garlic Oil Roasted Potatoes (page 172), these quick pickles are done just inside of an hour and are great to have on hand whenever you need them. They're good stored in the refrigerator for about a week; after that, you might want to cook them down with a little butter and a good dose of sugar to create a pickled red onion marmalade (running for Sandwich Spread of the Year in our house). As a matter of fact, try roughly chopping and sautéing those potatoes in garlic oil, topping them with some of these onions, and finishing with a little cream, salt and pepper, and you've got a killer hash for breakfast in about 5 minutes. And, of course, no one will judge you harshly if you decide to fry up a couple of eggs with that chimichurri compound butter we mentioned on page 164. The quantities listed below are to be used as a guide. This recipe can be easily scaled up or down, and once you get the hang of it, no measuring is required.

Makes 3 cups

3 large red onions, sliced ¼ inch thick
½ cup granulated sugar
1½ tablespoons kosher salt
1 cup red wine vinegar

Place the sliced onions in a large bowl and toss them to coat well with the sugar, then lightly toss with the salt. Leave them uncovered, at room temperature, for about 20 minutes to wilt.

Pour in the red wine vinegar and toss occasionally over the next 40 minutes to an hour.

Taste and adjust the sugar and salt to taste. Once the onions have softened and turned a bright purple-pink, drain them in a colander to remove the excess marinade. Use immediately or transfer to an airtight container and refrigerate for about 1 week.

CLARIFIED BUTTER

NV A: We use clarified butter when we want to cook something on high heat but still allowing for the amazing flavor that only butter contains. The "smoke point" is the issue in "high heat cookery." While olive oil and extra-virgin olive oil have wonderful flavor we prize, one simply cannot heat it up very high without it burning. The most famous use we have for clarified butter is when we cook the Black Betty's Pan-Cooked Yellowtail (page 84). It was the way I was taught to make the dish and the butter restates the silken butter nature of the overall presentation of that dish.

Makes 1½ cups
1 pound unsalted butter

Place the butter in a heavy saucepan over a medium-high heat. When a blond foam forms, gently skim it off and discard, taking care not to skim any precious butter with it. Continue until no more foam forms. Remove from the heat and let the butter settle, but do not let it cool.

Place a cheesecloth over a strainer and the strainer over a bowl. Ladle the clear and nearly golden butter through the cheesecloth, taking care not to disturb any milk solids at the bottom of the pan. Discard the milk solids.

Carefully transfer the clarified butter to a non-reactive dish and let cool. Refrigerate for up to 3 months.

SMOKEY OVEN-ROASTED TOMATOES

NVA: For roasted tomatoes that taste as if they've been smoked, use this easy and quick recipe. I like to serve them with any grilled meat or fish, or try them with the Shrimp Annatto on page 30. Swap these out for the fresh or canned tomatoes with which you would usually make your red pasta sauce and get amazing compliments.

Makes 3 cups

2½ pounds ripe, in-season tomatoes, sliced in half and deseeded
1 tablespoon smoked pimentón
½ tablespoon kosher salt
½ tablespoon freshly ground black pepper
3½ tablespoons extra-virgin olive oil, for drizzling
2½ tablespoons sherry wine vinegar, for drizzling

Preheat the oven to 275°F. Line a sheet pan with parchment paper.

Arrange the tomato slices, cut side up, on the prepared pan.

In a small bowl, stir together the pimentón, salt and pepper. Season the cut sides of the tomatoes evenly with the spice rub. Drizzle with the oil and vinegar and roast in the oven until the tomato skins begin to pull away from the tomatoes, 30 to 40 minutes. Remove the tomatoes from the oven and let cool.

When cool enough to handle, peel away the tomato skins and discard. The smokey tomatoes can be chopped or blended, depending on how you intend to use them. Use immediately or transfer to several airtight containers or zip-tight plastic bags and refrigerate for up to 2 weeks or freeze for up to 3 months.

Cooking Note: This recipe is completely scalable, so feel free to adapt to any amount of tomatoes you want to roast.

CONCH LINGO

Bijol: A spice and herb mix developed in Cuba in the 1920s to season rice for a yellow appearance, as if the much more expensive saffron had been used.

Buches: Individual sips of Cuban coffee served in tiny plastic thimble cups.

Bubbas/Bubbaism: Key West locals and their ways; Bubba System: A mysterious, sometimes fair, localized system of doing favors, whereby things either just get done—or won't happen at all.

Conch: *Strombus gigas Linne* in the Latin, it refers to both the mollusk that used to be free to take out of the ocean here but now is protected as well as the folks that are born in Key West . . . less protected but equally tropical.

Cracked Conch: A preparation of conch meat that has been sliced thinly (like scallopine), pounded and bread-crumbed before being pan-cooked.

Coconut Telegraph: What most of North America might call the "grapevine" or what Spanish-speakers might call *la chusma*, it refers to the word on the street, and is a vital part of understanding what's happening in town.

Duval Crawl: Drinking one's way up or down Duval Street, frequenting as many bars as one can manage.

Florida Lobsters: Also known as "crawfish," they are the clawless variety of lobster found in the waters of the Caribbean.

Island Time: Key West is a culture dedicated to delay. You can set your watch on it; Mañanaism: Variation on island time, it comes from the Spanish *manana*, meaning "tomorrow."

Johnnycake: A corruption of "journey cake" in all likelihood, is any kind of bread taken out on a boat journey.

Mile Markers: Little green signs that dot the side of the road up and down the Overseas Highway. Locals use them to easily refer to a location's position in relation to US1.

Overseas Highway: A chain of bridges and island highways connecting the Florida Keys to the U.S. mainland for travel by automobile. Before the highway was built, there was a railroad built by Henry Flagler that was destroyed by a hurricane. Before that, the keys were only reachable by ship.

Sunset Celebration: Mallory Square is where folks gather nightly for a party that peaks when the sun descends into the Gulf of Mexico and folks applaud and holler in appreciation. You won't want to miss the entertainment or the mesmerizing colors of the Key West sky when it happens.

HANGOUTS

DUVAL & DOWNTOWN

The Green Parrot Bar
601 Whitehead Street
Key West, FL 33040
www.greenparrot.com

Captain Tony's Saloon
428 Greene Street
Key West, FL 33040
www.capttonyssaloon.com

Sloppy Joe's
201 Duval Street
Key West, FL 33040
www.sloppyjoes.com

The Conch Shop
308 Petronia Street
Key West, FL 33040
(305) 292-5005

La Crêperie
300 Petronia Street
Key West, FL 33040
www.lacreperiekeywest.com

PLACES IN THE HOODS

Johnson's Grocery
800 Thomas Street
Key West, FL 33040
(305) 294-8680

Blue Heaven
729 Thomas Street
Key West, FL 33040
www.blueheavenkw.com

5 Brothers Grocery
930 Southard Street
Key West, FL 33040
www.5brothersgrocery.
tripod.com

El Siboney Restaurant
900 Catherine Street
Key West, FL 33040
www.elsiboneyrestaurant.com

Sandy's Café
1026 White Street
Key West, FL 33040
(305) 295-0159

The Elk's Club
1107 Whitehead Street
Key West, FL 33040
(305) 896-5514

PLACES ON THE WATER

The Pier House
1 Duval Street
Key West, FL 33040
www.pierhouse.com

Louie's Backyard
700 Waddell Avenue
Key West, FL 33040
www.louiesbackyard.com

Half Shell Raw Bar
231 Margaret Street
Key West, FL 33040
www.halfshellrawbar.com

OUT OF TOWN

Hogfish Bar and Grill
6810 Front Street
Stock Island, FL 33040
www.hogfishbar.com

Robert Is Here Fruit Stand
19200 Southwest 344th Street
Homestead, FL 33034
www.robertishere.com

INDEX

NVA: Thanks go to—

The Renegade Conch Spirit in all of its indefinable crazy, wonderful, sweet, "only in Key West" way.
The teams at Tuyo, Miami, and NORMAN'S at The Ritz-Carlton, Grande Lakes, Orlando.
Anja Schmidt, this book is bound and guided by you.
Penny De Los Santos, you have "more light" than any photographer I know.
Dennis Hayes, my coconut kindred-spirited agent, publisher, friend.
Steve Harris and Jeff Hagel, my lifelong Illinois-Key West Brothers.
Family Love to Buddy, Annie, Jane, Bet and Cayce.
The Yaber family, who have welcomed us with brazos abiertos!
The Amsler family, across the generations and from heaven.

JVA: Thanks go to—

The Conch Republic, the idiosyncratic, gentle, stubborn, devil-may-care place that she is, was, and ever
will be. It may just be a Rock between the Ocean and the Gulf, but it's our Rock.
My first friends, the Perrys, with whom I shared this Island Home in our earliest years.
My old and dear friends La Familia: Aimee, Kimmy, Stiffy, Jimi, Frank, and Bryan. Our crew is smaller
and in some ways stronger than ever. I love all you guys.
The De La Paz and Hans families, R.I.P. Derek and Andrew, my fallen brothers, I will miss you always.
Brad, Lashonda, Zion, and Tyler Denis, thank you for choosing us as family.
Chefs Todd Meuller and Giordano Marchese, in just a few months, the two of you helped to instill in me a
breadth of knowledge and a skill set that serve me every day of my life. I honor your teachings and think of you
both every time I step into a kitchen.
Travis Starwalt and his family: Troy, Melinda, Julie, and Russ. How you all get along without him around
every is a mystery... R.I.P. Mark. I wish I could thank you in person. Your son is a shining light.